Female Offenders: Meeting Needs of a Neglected Population

The following articles were originally published in the
Federal Bureau of Prisons' Spring 1992 *Federal Prisons Journal*:

A Profile of Female Offenders in State and Federal Prisons
Equality or Difference?
Alderson: The Early Years
From Victim to Victimizer
HIV, AIDS, and the Female Offender
Care of the Pregnant Offender
The Older Female Offender
Turning Up the Lights
The 5-South Unit at MCC New York
Canada's Federal System for Female Offenders

Perry M. Johnson, President
James A. Gondles, Jr., Executive Director
Patricia L. Poupore, Director of Communications and Publications
Elizabeth Watts, Publications Managing Editor
Jennifer A. Nichols, Project Editor
Marianna Nunan, Associate Editor
Kristen Miller, Contributing Editor
Kristen Mosbaek, Cover Design
Cover Photos: Craig Crawford and Kevin Reilly, U.S. Department of Justice

ISBN 0-929310-86-1

Printed in the United States of America by United Book Press, Inc., Baltimore,
Md.

This publication may be ordered from:
American Correctional Association
8025 Laurel Lakes Court
Laurel, MD 20707-5075
1-800-825-BOOK

Contents

Foreword

An ever-increasing number of offenders in today's correctional institutions has not only resulted in more men in U.S. prisons and jails, but also in an increasing number of women. In fact, the female offender population is growing at a higher rate than the male population, bringing to the forefront issues that must be addressed when supervising and handling this population. A need has also developed for a greater understanding of the impact incarceration has on women and on society in general.

The issues associated with supervising women in institutions designed and managed predominantly by men has always posed a challenge to correctional staff and administrators. Although some institutions have been designed specifically for women, most have not. The inherent differences that exist between the two sexes create difficulty in managing them equally and with fairness.

Historically, the question of whether to treat incarcerated women equally, differently, or different but equally has perplexed correctional administrators. Today, it is believed that different programs for different needs are necessary, and administrators at all levels are beginning to share and discover the best ways to handle female inmates and their particular concerns.

In this book of readings, eighteen valuable articles deal with the unique problems associated with managing female inmates. This informative publication will not only be of great interest to correctional administrators and staff, but will also help academicians, students, and the general public gain a better understanding and awareness of the complex issues associated with incarcerating more and more female offenders.

Special thanks go to the authors, who contributed freely of their knowledge and time. The Federal Bureau of Prisons is gratefully acknowledged for allowing republication of ten articles, which first appeared in the *Federal Prisons Journal*.

James A. Gondles, Jr.
Executive Director
American Correctional Association

I.

A Profile of Female Offenders in State and Federal Prisons

by Sue Kline

In the decade 1981-91, the number of women in the Federal Bureau of Prisons' custody steadily increased. In 1981, slightly more than 1,400 women were held in federal facilities. By 1991, female inmates numbered more than 5,000, representing a 254 percent increase during the ten-year period. The rate of growth for the number of men held during the same period was 147 percent, from 24,780 in 1981 to 61,208 in 1991. In June 1992, the bureau held 5,103 women in its facilities—7.4 percent of the 68,779 inmates then being housed.

The female prison population grew at a faster rate than the male population in seven of the ten years between 1981 and 1991. While the number of female inmates has been increasing, the proportion of the population they represent has also been on the rise. In 1981, women made up 5.4 percent of the bureau's inmate population. By 1991, they represented 7.6 percent of the inmates. By comparison, in state prison populations, the proportion of women in 1991 was 5.6 percent. The rate of growth for the number of female inmates in state facilities exceeded that for males in each year since 1981. From 1980 to 1989, the male population increased by 112 percent, while the female population increased by 202 percent (Bureau of Justice Statistics 1992).

The 5,103 women in bureau custody in June 1992 were housed in thirteen facilities—six of which were all-female facilities, while the other seven included both male and female units, primarily in detention facilities. The largest all-female facility is the Federal Medical Center in Lexington, Kentucky, the primary medical center for female inmates where more than 1,800 women (36 percent of all female inmates) are held. The next largest all-female facility is the Federal Prison Camp in Alderson, West Virginia, currently housing 809 women, or 15.2 percent of the federal female inmate population. Alderson was the first institution for federal female offenders; it opened in 1927.

Offenses

In 1991, almost 64 percent of women in federal custody were serving time for a

Sue Kline is a research analyst in the Federal Bureau of Prisons Office of Research and Evaluation.

drug-related offense—most commonly for the manufacture or distribution of illegal drugs. The next most common identifiable offenses were property offenses, such as larceny or theft (6.3 percent), and extortion, bribery, or fraud offenses (6.2 percent). The offense type of today's female offender differs from that of the female offender of ten years ago. In 1981, most female offenders were being held for property offenses (28.2 percent). The next most common identifiable offenses in 1981 were drug offenses (26.0 percent), robbery (11.8 percent), and white-collar offenses (7.6 percent).

The offense profile of men held in federal facilities in 1991 shows that the majority of them (55.8 percent) were also being held for drug offenses. The next most common identifiable offense for men was robbery (12.2 percent). The male population also saw a decrease in the proportion of robbery, property, white-collar, and immigration offenders between 1981 and 1991. Both men and women showed increases in the proportion of drug offenders and a small increase in the proportion of arms, explosives, courts and corrections, and national security offenders.

The latest offense-specific information for women housed in state institutions shows them most likely to be housed for a property or violent offense (81.9 percent). These 1986 figures from the Bureau of Justice Statistics (BJS) show that only 12 percent of women housed in state facilities were there for a drug-related offense. Fifty-nine percent of the women in state institutions were sentenced for a nonviolent crime, 17 percent for fraud, 15 percent for larceny or theft, and 5 percent for public-order offenses, such as commercial vice or weapons violations (BJS 1991).

Characteristics

The female population housed in bureau facilities as of June 1992 had characteristics similar to the male population. A majority of inmates were white and not of Hispanic origin. The distribution of ages was similar for men and women, though the average age for men was 37.3—slightly higher than that for women, which was thirty-six.

The latest figures from BJS show that state inmates are noticeably younger and more likely to be black than those in federal prisons. In state prisons in 1986, 72 percent of men and 73 percent of women were under the age of 35.3. A majority of the women (46.1 percent) and men (45.3 percent) were black.

In June 1992, every state in the union was represented by women incarcerated in Bureau of Prisons facilities. More than 91 percent of women had as their place of residence a U.S. state, territory, or the District of Columbia, leaving 8.8 percent as non-U.S. citizens. More than 11 percent of the female inmates had Florida as their state of residence. The other top states were California (11.1 percent), Texas (9.8 percent), New York (9.2 percent), and Illinois (3.5 percent). The top five states of residence for male inmates are California (12.3 percent), Florida (11.3 percent), Texas (8.9 percent), New York (8.4 percent), and Illinois (3.7 percent).

The tables on the following pages compare statistics for federal and state inmates.

PRISON POPULATION BY SEX

YEARS	FEDERAL			STATE AND FEDERAL		
	Female	Male	% Female	Female	Male	% Female
1981	1,415	24,780	5.4	15,537	354,393	4.2
1982	1,519	26,614	5.4	17,785	396,021	4.3
1983	1,722	28,492	5.7	19,020	417,835	4.4
1984	1,842	30,475	5.7	20,798	441,208	4.5
1985	2,183	33,859	6.1	23,148	479,359	4.6
1986	2,741	38,771	6.6	26,531	518,441	4.9
1987	3,058	41,911	6.8	29,123	555,961	5.0
1988	2,949	41,730	6.6	32,592	594,996	5.2
1989	3,635	48,213	7.0	40,556	669,498	5.7
1990	4,263	55,025	7.2	NA	NA	NA
1991	5,006	61,208	7.6	NA	NA	NA
June 1992	5,103	63,676	7.4	NA	NA	NA

Data for 1981-1991 are for September of each year.
NA = not available

OFFENSE OF INMATES BY SEX (%)
IN FEDERAL INSTITUTIONS

	1981		1991	
	Female	Male	Female	Male
Drug offenses	26.0	26.3	63.9	55.8
Robbery	11.8	24.2	4.4	12.2
Property offenses	28.2	14.9	6.3	4.5
Extortion, bribery, fraud	5.1	5.2	6.2	4.9
Violent offenses	7.1	8.2	2.0	3.8
D.C. offenses	NR	NR	3.4	2.2
Arms, explosives, arson	1.0	4.2	2.1	5.0
White-collar offenses	7.6	3.4	2.6	1.3
Immigration	3.6	5.0	0.6	0.9
Courts or corrections	1.2	0.7	1.3	0.8
Sex offenses	0.1	0.5	0.1	0.5
National security	0.0	0.0	0.1	0.1
Miscellaneous	8.5	7.3	7.0	7.9

NR = not reported separately
Note: Percentages may not add to 100 due to rounding. Data are for September of each year. 1981 data include sixteen unsentenced female inmates and 101 unsentenced male inmates. The offense listed is the one with the longest sentence length.

MOST SERIOUS OFFENSE OF FEMALE INMATES
IN STATE INSTITUTIONS (%), 1979 and 1986

	Percentage of Female State Prison Inmates	
	1979 Total	1986 Total
Most serious offense	100.0	100.0
VIOLENT OFFENSES	48.9	40.7
Murder*	15.5	13.0
Negligent manslaughter	9.8	6.8
Kidnapping	1.4	0.9
Rape	0.4	0.2
Other sexual assault	0.3	0.9
Robbery	13.6	10.6
Assault	7.6	7.1
Other violent	0.4	1.2
PROPERTY OFFENSES	36.8	41.2
Burglary	5.3	5.9
Larceny/theft	11.2	14.7
Motor vehicle theft	0.5	0.5
Arson	1.2	1.2
Fraud	17.3	17.0
Stolen property	0.9	1.6
Other property	0.4	0.4
DRUG OFFENSES	10.5	12.0
Possession	2.7	4.0
Trafficking	7.1	7.3
Other drug/unspecified	0.7	0.7
PUBLIC-ORDER OFFENSES	2.9	5.1
Weapons	0.9	0.9
Other public-order	2.0	4.3
OTHER OFFENSES	0.9	0.9

*Includes nonnegligent manslaughter.

Note: May not add to 100 percent because of rounding. Offense data were available for at least 99 percent of the inmates in 1986 and 1979.

Source: Bureau of Justice Statistics

FEDERAL INMATE CHARACTERISTICS BY SEX, JUNE 1992

Characteristic	Female (%)	Male (%)
Age (years)		
18-25	13.2	12.2
26-30	19.2	16.8
31-35	20.9	19.2
36-40	18.9	17.8
41-45	12.2	14.3
46-50	8.0	8.7
51-55	4.0	5.2
56-60	1.9	3.1
61-65	1.0	1.7
Older than 65	0.6	1.1
Average age	36.0	37.3
Race		
White	58.7	64.9
Black	39.1	32.5
Native American	1.0	1.6
Asian	1.2	1.1
Ethnicity		
Hispanic	24.9	26.2
Non-Hispanic	75.1	73.8

Note: Percentages may not add to 100 due to rounding.

STATE INMATE CHARACTERISTICS BY SEX, 1986

Characteristic	Female (%)	Male (%)
Age (years)		
17 or younger	0.2	0.5
18-24	22.3	26.9
25-34	50.5	45.5
35-44	19.6	19.4
45-54	5.5	5.2
55-64	1.5	1.9
65 or older	0.4	0.6
Race and ethnicity		
White non-Hispanic	39.6	39.5
Black non-Hispanic	46.1	45.3
Hispanic	11.7	12.6
Other race*	2.5	2.5

*Includes American Indians, Alaskan, Natives, Asians, and Pacific Islanders.

Conclusion

The number of female inmates in state and federal institutions has increased over the last decade, as has their proportion of the total prison population. While the greatest number of federal female inmates were committed for a drug-related offense, state inmates' committment offenses were equally divided between violent and nonviolent offenses, with a smaller number committed for a drug-related offense. Female inmates in both state and federal systems are most likely to be twenty-five to thirty-five years of age. While most federal inmates are white and non-Hispanic, state inmates are more likely to be black and non-Hispanic.

Results from an in-depth survey of federal inmates, conducted in conjunction with a BJS survey of state inmates in 1991, will soon provide us with more detailed comparisons for male and female inmates across systems. Whether they are state or federal; black, white, or Hispanic; or committed for a drug, violent, or property offense, female offenders share many of the same problems and concerns, which will be addressed in the following chapters.

References

Bureau of Justice Statistics. 1991. Women in prison. *Bureau of Justice Statistics Special Report (March).*

Bureau of Justice Statistics. 1992. Prisoners in 1991. *Bureau of Justice Statistics Bulletin* (May).

II.

Equality or Difference?

by Nicole Hahn Rafter

Over time, women in U.S. jails and prisons have been incarcerated under enormously varied conditions. However, one question has remained constant: Should female inmates be treated like male inmates or differently?

The current situation is complicated by the growing realization that outwardly equal treatment often means less adequate care for women. It does so because the standard is set on male terms that overlook important gender differences. Today, we are seeing a search for new policies that can achieve equality while taking gender differences into account.

Equal Treatment

When the first state prisons were founded at the end of the eighteenth century, there were (as there are today) fewer women in prison than men. With only one, three, or ten female inmates, states had no need for a separate women's institution. They began by operating just one prison or penitentiary to which all felons were sent, regardless of sex. In these early institutions, women were often celled next door to men. Outwardly, they received the same treatment. But this seeming equality, in fact, meant more difficult circumstances for women, as the following examples illustrate:

1. The few female inmates were surrounded by men. This created privacy problems and meant that they were more lonely than their male counterparts. It also made women more vulnerable to sexual exploitation by guards and male inmates.
2. All the staff were male, not only the guards but the physicians and chaplains. Visitors from the outside, like the guards on the inside, identified more closely with the male than the female inmates. For visiting physicians and chaplains, as for members of their broader culture, women belonged on a pedestal; thus, if a woman "fell," she fell

Nicole Hahn Rafter is a professor at the College of Criminal Justice, Northeastern University, and is the author of Partial Justice: Women, Prisons and Social Control *(Transaction Publishers, 1990, 2d ed.).*

A version of this article was presented at a Federal Bureau of Prisons "Issues Forum" in June 1991.

farther than any man and must consequently be far more depraved. Therefore, physicians and chaplains often steered clear of female inmates, giving more attention to male inmates.

3. If a female inmate in one of these early prisons was pregnant, she had to deliver the baby alone, in her cell. Predictably, infant death rates were very high. Male inmates did not have to contend with such problems.

As the decades passed and the number of female inmates increased, they were moved to separate quarters, perhaps a small cellblock in a corner of the prison yard or, toward the middle of the nineteenth century, to a separate unit just outside the wall. Removal brought some advantages. Female inmates were no longer isolated from other women and were less vulnerable to sexual exploitation.

But removal also took a toll. The farther women were located from the center of the prison, the less access they had to whatever opportunities were available to the male inmates, such as medical advice, religious services, and opportunities to exercise in the yard. The isolated women's units had no kitchens. Food was carried to them from the men's quarters, often just once a day, and the food usually arrived cold. If the warden did not hire a matron to supervise the women's quarters, female inmates had no protection from one another. There are records of some wild fights in these early women's units.

In sum, during this first stage in women's prison history, from roughly 1790 to 1870, the policy was to treat female and male inmates alike. But because the norms were set by male officers with reference to the needs of the far larger number of male inmates, outward equality in fact produced inferior conditions for incarcerated women.

Differential Treatment

The situation began to change about 1870 as the idea of rehabilitation took hold. Interest grew in reforming female as well as male inmates. However, due to the "separate spheres" doctrine, according to which men are best fit for public work while women are inherently better at dealing with domestic tasks, children, and other women, the job of reforming female inmates was relegated to other women: middle-class reformers.

This task was welcomed by late nineteenth-century feminists, who threw themselves into the task of establishing separate women's reformatories. These middle-class women succeeded in the often difficult job of persuading all-male legislatures to fund separate reformatory prisons for women. When the new reformatories opened, these reformers frequently became the administrators.

The reformers established the principle that women in prison must be treated entirely different from male inmates. Copying the model of the juvenile reformatory, they built the new women's prisons on the cottage plan. Inmates lived in relatively small "cottages," or individual units, where they could be supervised by motherly matrons.

Programmatically, the new women's reformatories were designed to rehabilitate by inculcating domesticity. While the programs included outdoor work, inmates were mainly trained to sew, cook, and wait on tables. At parole, they were sent to positions as domestic servants, where they could be supervised by yet other middle-class women.

In short, the regimen of the first separate penal institutions for women was infantilizing: inmates were treated as wayward children rather than responsible adults who, after release, would have to live independently. The reformers did not face the fact that most of their charges would have to support themselves. Alderson, the first federal women's prison, was built during this period. Like its state counterparts, Alderson adhered to the principle that women should be treated differently than men.

Differential treatment manifested itself in sentencing practices as well as in architecture and programs. The reformers who founded the state reformatories for women had little interest in dealing with felons—serious offenders who were also often black. The reformers preferred to direct their rehabilitative efforts toward minor offenders with whom they could identify—white women found guilty of misdemeanors or (more frequently) offenses against chastity. The new women's reformatories held these minor offenders on long sentences—terms equivalent to those imposed on felons in state penitentiaries.

Thus, differential treatment carried its own set of liabilities:

1. Women held in women's reformatories were forced into a "true woman" mold of domesticity that infantilized and ill-prepared them for self-support in an industrialized society.
2. Moreover, women who committed minor offenses were now held on long sentences—much longer than the sentences served by men who committed minor offenses.
3. And, of course, men were never sent to state prisons for violations of chastity. The women's prison system became a means of enforcing the double standard of sexual morality.

The idea of differential treatment of male and female inmates prevailed through the early 1960s, a persistence illustrated by a recommendation that a certain women's prison develop a dairy industry. Milking cows, the formulator of this policy argued, is an excellent activity for female inmates because women have a natural affinity for udders!

The women's movement of the late 1960s brought a reaction against such talk, however, and renewed demands for equal treatment of male and female inmates. The tide began to turn against domestic training. Instead, advocates insisted on programs that would prepare released women for real-world jobs and self-support.

Another signal of the shift back to the idea of equal treatment was a wave of litigation against differential care. In the late 1960s, female inmates began using the courts to challenge sentencing laws that made them liable to longer terms than male inmates who had similar records and conviction offenses.

Today—Taking Gender Differences into Account

We are all familiar with aspects of the drive toward women's equal rights. But many people are unaware that it has been accompanied by a growing perception that equal treatment usually means less adequate treatment. The following examples illustrate a new awareness that gender differences must be taken into account:

1. Law libraries. Incarcerated women are finally being given law libraries as adequate as those available to incarcerated men. But because women have no tradition of "jailhouse lawyering," they are less skilled in using legal resources. Thus, several recent court decisions have ordered not only adequate law libraries, but legal training for female inmates, so that their level of access to the courts will in fact equal that of male inmates. These decisions recognize that equality involves parity—actual as well as apparent equivalence.
2. Children. A second, very different, example of the need to recognize gender differences concerns children. Unlike incarcerated men, most women in prison leave behind children who are solely dependent on them. Every study of this matter concludes that separation from children constitutes a major hardship for incarcerated women. The studies show that separation is also devastating for the children, who must keep in contact with their primary parent if they are to avoid severe psychological damage. Thus, although male and female inmates are both separated from their children, this situation affects them differently and has different social consequences.

Developing a New Model

Today, the two major historical themes of equal and differential treatment are flowing together. Those involved with planning for female inmates are trying to deal with both considerations simultaneously.

This confluence signals an awareness that neither approach works well on its own. Outwardly even-handed treatment produces inferior treatment for incarcerated women because the norm is still set by male administrators, working with male needs uppermost in mind. Deliberately differential treatment alone also spells inferior treatment, for it reinforces the gender division of labor.

Policy makers are seeking ways to go *beyond* both the equality and difference models. The move is emphatically not toward merely combining the two approaches, for the result would be to compound their individual disadvantages. Rather, the search is for a way, or ways, to transcend the traditional approaches by developing a new model. This new model will no doubt borrow the best elements of the two older approaches. But it will also have to find ways of avoiding their inherent drawbacks. As yet, we do not know what the new model will look like. We do know that merely extending the older approaches will perpetuate a tradition that began to form on the day the first state prison received its first female offender. That tradition, whether based on the idea of similar treatment or differential treatment, has been one of automatically condemning incarcerated women to inferior care.

III.

Differences That Make a Difference: Managing a Women's Correctional Institution

by Charles Turnbo

My job as associate warden at the U.S. Penitentiary in Lompoc, California, provided excellent training for my next assignment as warden at the Federal Correctional Institution in Pleasanton, California. It's only 300 miles from the penitentiary in Lompoc to the Federal Correctional Institution in Pleasanton, and both prisons house high security inmates. However, there is one very important difference between the two facilities: Pleasanton is an all-female facility.

Pleasanton opened in July 1974 as the federal minimum security facility for male and female juveniles. In July 1977, it was converted to an all-female federal correctional institution, housing all security levels. The "high security unit" at the Federal Correctional Institution, Alderson, West Virginia, was phased out. A number of lifers and serious disciplinary cases were transferred at that time to Pleasanton. It was the end of the line for female disciplinary cases and offered the high security features needed for the cadre of lifers and high security inmates. In February 1980, a decline in the number of female offenders led to the institution's conversion back to a co-correctional facility for men and women of all security levels. In October 1990, the facility was re-established as an all-female institution for all security levels, with a minimum security satellite camp for men adjacent to the institution outside the fences.

I served as warden at Pleasanton between 1978 and 1984, during a time when female offenders were the focus of much attention. The Bureau of Prisons held its historic Conference on the Confinement of Female Offenders in March 1978 at the Federal Correctional Institution in Lexington, Kentucky. The national women's movement had begun to focus attention on women in jails and prisons. The Women's Bureau of the U.S. Department of Labor was spearheading "nontraditional" job training programs for women, including those detained in prisons. Civil rights litigation was addressing female inmate rights on a wide variety of issues. The Congressional Subcommittee on Courts, Civil Liberties, and the Administration of Justice held public hearings on the female offender. Pleasanton's most publicized inmate, newspaper heiress Patty Hearst, also brought much attention to the institution and its residents.

It was an exciting and challenging experience serving as warden of this all-

Charles Turnbo is the regional director for the South Central Region of the Federal Bureau of Prisons in Dallas, Texas.

female facility. Looking back, there were many good lessons learned that can now be shared. I learned more about correctional management and human behavior in that six years as warden than in all my other eight assignments put together! Some of these lessons were taught by staff there, others by the inmates, some by my superiors, and a few by the courts. Some of the issues concerning female offenders have changed, but many still confront those in correctional management. At the 1991 female offenders conference, many of the same conference topics discussed at the 1978 conference were addressed: transporting female inmates, the possible need for a separate inmate classification system for women, the geographic displacement of female inmates, pregnant inmates and care of newborn infants, programs for female offenders, training for staff who work with female inmates, and women's health issues. Over this thirteen-year period we have made progress in addressing these and other issues concerning female inmates.

Initial Impressions

Many wardens want nothing to do with an all-female prison population. I received as many condolences as congratulations when I was promoted to warden at Pleasanton. My colleagues who had prior experience with female inmates shared their war stories with me. Even on my brief orientation visit to Pleasanton, I was repeatedly warned about the "dangers" that awaited me in the new job.

I agree with Dr. Esther Heffernan (1978), who says, "Women are seen as a persistent and continuing problem in corrections for two reasons: one, their small numbers, and two, their perceived nature." Over the next few months, I learned that much of the hand-wringing and horror stories about female inmates were myths.

There are some well-established differences between male and female inmates. The women are much more talkative to staff. They display their emotions openly (as a new warden, I found that a nearby supply of tissue was a necessity). Women have more suicidal thoughts and have suffered more physical and sexual abuse than men. Female inmates are much more vocal about family and children's issues and many still consider themselves to be the primary caretakers of their children, even though they are incarcerated. Health issues receive much more attention among female offenders, and they present many challenges in the areas of birth control, pregnancy, childbirth, child placement, and abortion. Finally, female inmates possess fewer job skills than their male counterparts, have shorter work histories, and are less educated. Based on my experience at Pleasanton, I encountered the following key differences in managing a women's versus a men's prison:

- staff-inmate rapport
- response to authority and confinement
- level of inmate participation in operations and programs
- inmate responsiveness to positive incentives

Staff-inmate Rapport

One striking difference between female and male inmates is their relationships with staff. Female inmates, on being released, often said goodbye to virtually every staff member in the institution. Many of the women had put down deep roots while in prison. Some had a hard time making the transition from prison to community living and wanted to return to Pleasanton. On their return to the facility, it was as if they had come back to a family reunion. And, to my surprise, they were often as glad to see the staff as their fellow inmates.

Close staff-inmate rapport had both positive and negative consequences. On the positive side, staff served as role models for some of the inmates. Close relationships also promoted good communication between staff and inmates. Also, it helped the teachers, chaplains, counselors, psychologists, and case managers who used this rapport as a vehicle to provide inmate services.

On the negative side, some inmates and staff took advantage of these special relationships in a destructive fashion. Sometimes staff were compromised by getting too close to an inmate; we also had inmates taken advantage of by a few staff members.

The unusual rapport between staff and inmates at Pleasanton made a number of things possible. Programs were in high demand and had excellent participation. Violence was virtually nonexistent. Everyone was well-informed.

However, I felt uncomfortable with some aspects of staff-inmate closeness. From time to time, there would be hugs between inmates and staff members. There were occasions when staff members would get together in the community with a former inmate, and there were several cases of romantic involvement between staff members and inmates.

It became a priority for us to work on professionalism (e.g., how staff members look, how they perform their jobs, and how they interact with inmates). Attention was given to staff professionalism through training as well as regular meetings. This put a healthy distance between staff members and inmates.

Response to Authority and Confinement

Another difference in managing female inmates versus their male counterparts dealt with their general response to confinement. I found that we often fostered and encouraged the women to be dependent on staff members by our behavior and our response to their behavior. Staff members often played the parent role to the inmates' childlike role in situations involving very manipulative female inmates.

During my first week on the job at Pleasanton, I had to deny a particular inmate a furlough. Within minutes of my decision, I heard wailing and screaming outside my office. When I inquired about the noise, the secretary calmly reported, "Oh, that's just the inmate whose furlough you turned down." Such behavior in the past had sometimes been used to "appeal" administrative decisions and get support from a sympathetic inmate population. We confronted such behavior and did not reverse our actions simply based on a well-staged temper tantrum.

Similarly, I soon learned that the warden was considered a medical expert and was often the source of a second opinion of the hospital staff's decisions. On one occasion, an inmate dashed into my office, lifted her examination gown, and demanded a second opinion. She was escorted to the detention unit where the medical staff completed their exam. She also was the subject of disciplinary action for her inappropriate behavior.

With the help of competent staff members, we worked at holding the inmates accountable for their behavior and actions. We spent a lot of time teaching personal responsibility to inmates. The results were encouraging. We observed a reduction in acting-out behavior and improvement in self-management. This had a beneficial effect on the operation of the whole facility. We used inmate communication committees to address issues and ideas. Staff agreed with many of the issues raised by the inmates as legitimate concerns. As a result, we spent less time dealing with immature, childish behavior and more time on self-help and positive self-improvement.

Inmate Participation

One impressive program underway during my time at Pleasanton was Project MATCH (Mothers And Their CHildren), which was co-sponsored by the National Council on Crime and Delinquency. This program operated within the institution to provide a children's center and several parenting programs for inmate mothers and their children. The program revealed a compelling partnership between the institution, the inmates, and a number of community volunteers and workers. The community showed strong support through the efforts of volunteers, donations, and grants.

The MATCH project demonstrated the best form of collaboration, communication, and coordination between inmates and staff members. Whether they were janitors, child care assistants, or participants, the inmates demonstrated the value of positive inmate participation. Several inmates were involved in the oversight board that helped steer the MATCH project. To their credit, the inmate participants helped us keep the program drug-free and effective.

Today, parenting and children's center programs are found at all major federal facilities for women. They have evolved from this original pilot initiative.

Inmate involvement in other areas helped us substantially improve operations and procedures. The inmates advised us on issues and concerns and were then better informed to make necessary policy changes.

One example in which we solicited inmate opinion dealt with official visitors and institution tours. We were getting a lot of negative feedback from the inmate population on the number and size of tour groups. We were holding open houses for the public as well as for selective audiences in the areas of law enforcement, university faculty members and students, chambers of commerce boards and members, and potential customers for Federal Prison Industries' products. Also, some of our high-profile inmates had large numbers of visitors from the press. We had begun to experience bad inmate behavior during visits by outside guests.

Input from inmates resulted in using inmate tour guides, when appropriate, and enlisting inmates to serve as speakers to visitors. We also created a "speakers' bureau" to go out into the community and speak on a wide range of topics. Visits were made to schools, churches, community civic clubs, and chambers of commerce. These events were very popular with inmates and the public as well. Over the next few weeks after the program began, inmate resistance to tours and official visitors dissipated. We developed an important partnership in the area of "public awareness."

The Pleasanton staff used inmate involvement effectively in solving day-to-day operational issues throughout the institution. In food service, the administrators would frequently try out new suggestions on a select group of inmates. Their feedback helped determine the fate of the proposed menu change.

Education, recreation, chapel, industrial, and work programs all found innovative uses of inmate involvement. We had meetings with the industries' inmates and would share productivity goals, rejected products, and employee information.

The results were very beneficial. Industrial profits, quality, morale, sanitation, and equipment upkeep all improved.

Positive Versus Negative Reinforcement

A fourth difference in managing a female population deals with their responsiveness to positive reinforcement. While this principle works with men as well, it was a powerful tool in our work at Pleasanton. We found that rewarding positive behavior and accomplishments had a profound effect on inmate morale. We had many different kinds of rewards for accomplishments made on the job in areas of education and recreation or for a significant personal achievement. We had awards ceremonies in which inmates were recognized by their peers and staff members. Photographs were a treasured award. Also, getting to go to the dining hall first or getting a ''day off'' were sought-after awards. Understanding the principle of positive reinforcement helped our staff market many initiatives and receive excellent results from inmates and resulted in a decrease in the use of negative sanctions or force.

Conclusion

The talented staff of Pleasanton took great pride in working with inmates. The early years of the all-female population at Pleasanton demonstrated that we could maintain a safe, productive, positive environment in spite of what skeptics asserted about the nature of all-female prisons. We had no escapes, very few assaults, no organized work or food strikes, no sabotage to the facility, and very few inmates detained in administrative detention/segregation. This record is even more remarkable when one considers that Pleasanton served as the bureau's highest security female facility during these years.

At that time, Pleasanton was fortunate to have a manageable population, an uncommon condition in most women's prisons today. Severe institutional crowding limits the administrator's ability to benefit from the factors I've outlined. However, I find in our various all-female facilities, these difference still exist in various forms when compared to men's prisons. These are differences that make a difference.

References

Heffernan, E. 1978. *Female corrections—History and analysis.* Paper presented at the Confinement of Female Offenders Conference. Lexington, Kentucky.

Federal Bureau of Prisons. 1978. *Proceedings from Conference on Confinement of Female Offenders.* Washington, D.C.: BOP.

Federal Bureau of Prisons. 1991. *Proceedings from Female Offenders Conference.* Washington, D.C.: BOP.

IV.

Alderson: The Early Years

by Esther Heffernan

James V. Bennett (1970), who was director of the Federal Bureau of Prisons (BOP) for twenty-seven years, says in his memoirs, "No one has really known what to do with the few women who are condemned to prison, least of all the federal government." He wonders why women, who make up an insignificant number of those incarcerated, are paid so much attention by the public and receive leniency, mercy, and favorable treatment in the courts and corrections.

The early publications of the BOP reflect that insignificance. Bureau staff and inmates were identified as men, and programs were directed toward men. Women were the exception, making up 3.9 percent of the inmates in 1930, and were designated a problem. With the creation of the bureau in 1930, women moved into a new status in federal corrections.

Alderson and the Founding of the BOP

Assistant Attorney General Mabel Walker Willebrandt played an important role in laying the groundwork for the BOP. By the end of her tenure in the Department of Justice, Willebrandt watched the political influence of women wane and her contributions attributed to others. She was denied the federal judgeship that she had expected as a reward for her competence, commitment, and loyalty. In 1929, in response to an editorial recommending that the newly formed bureau be taken out of her jurisdiction, she wired Attorney General William D. Mitchell (Brown 1984):

> I think you owe it to me to make a statement of facts...that it is due solely to my labor and vision that the prison bureau is reclassified into a scientific major bureau...As a monument to my hard work...a first offender's reformatory has been established at Chillicothe...a modern women's institution established at Alderson...and industries started at

Esther Heffernan is a professor of sociology at Edgewood College, Madison, Wisconsin.

Editor's note: This chapter is an excerpt from a larger work titled "Banners, Brothels, and a 'Ladies Seminary': Women and Federal Corrections," to be included in an upcoming book, Escaping Prison Myth: Selected Topics in the History of Federal Corrections, *edited by John W. Roberts and published by American University Press.*

Leavenworth...I can no longer endure the belittling of my part in every accomplishment resulting from years of devoted labor...[and it is] unjust to give you, a newcomer to the whole problem, sole credit and picture me as a danger to prisons.

Alderson, the first federal institution for women and Willebrandt's "monument," opened in 1927, predating the founding of the BOP by three years. Located in rural West Virginia, Alderson consisted of fourteen cottages (offenders were segregated by race) built in a horseshoe pattern on two-tiered slopes. Each contained a kitchen and rooms for about thirty women. Male inmates brought from Leavenworth and Atlanta were housed in an adjoining camp to help finance the institution at a cost of $2.5 million.

In his memoirs, Bennett attributed the passage of appropriations for Alderson to President Calvin Coolidge's recommendation in his State of the Union Address with no menton of Willebrandt's role.

In the first year of operation before its formal opening on 14 November 1928, 174 women had been sent to Alderson from state prisons and jails. One hundred nineteen of them were drug law violators; only fifteen had violated prohibition laws, despite the myth that Alderson opened its doors with moonshining women from the hills of West Virginia. According to Congressional testimony in 1929, 70 to 80 percent of the women were suffering from social diseases and were unable to work in the dairy and the kitchens until they were cured. Thus, hospitalization rather than industry appeared to be the first need at Alderson.

At that time, the few federal wardens operated largely independently; it was not until several years after the founding of the new agency that the director was able to exercise effective control over them. One of the most independent-minded wardens was Alderson's Mary Belle Harris. In her autobiography *I Knew Them in Prison* (1936), Harris describes the development of an individualized classification system and the institution of inmate self-government with co-operative clubs. She insisted that the "warders" in each cottage be included in the decision-making and the classification process. Educational classes began (segregated by race for the 20 percent "colored"), ranging from English and arithmetic to table service, elementary agriculture, stenography, and typewriting. Also included were Bible study, elementary Americanization (developed for immigrants), and advanced Americanization that stressed civics and home economics.

Determined that drug addicts were not hopeless, Harris emphasized the need for withdrawal under medical supervision and individualized treatment under the joint watch of the staff and the inmate members of the co-operative clubs. Bird and tree clubs, pageants and plays, athletic teams, and well-censored movies enlivened leisure hours after the women's work on the dairy farm, on the cottages and grounds, and in Alderson's garment industry.

Harris quotes an inmate as saying: "This is the goin'est place I ever saw." With an annual country fair that exhibited the works of the cottages, the industries, and the farm, Harris brought the local community, as well as the members of the advisory board, into her open institution.

In fact, the excellent treatment and wonderful programs of the female offenders led Representative William F. Kopp to wonder in the 1929 Congressional hearings "whether or not it would rather unfit them for meeting the world—when you send them back to the household duties of ordinary homes...they might lose courage and want to get back to Alderson again."

According to Lekkerkerker (1931), "it is undoubtedly the largest and best equipped reformatory that exists." However, she voiced some concerns that are still heard today. They included: the heterogeneity of the population, which included white, black, Indian, Mexican, and Asian women; the nature of federal offenses, which brought a large number of drug addicts to the institution; and the distance the women were removed from their communities, which made it difficult for them to see their families.

In his 1928 report on the Federal Penal and Correctional Problem for the U.S. Bureau of Efficiency (now the Office of Management and Budget), Bennett described Alderson as a complete and self-sufficient institution capable of adequately caring for all federal female offenders for some years to come. He praised the "modern" facility as representing the best thought in penological methods.

In Bennett's discussion of the need for specialized federal institutions for men, he noted that Alderson's cottage plan permitted individual treatment of women by segregating them into groups and cottages by classes or types. However, he posed a question that became a major point of contention and a continuing issue in the bureau: "Will [the Federal Industrial Institution for Women] be able to successfully handle all the women who are committed to it?"

SchWeber's (1982) research on the early history of Alderson summarizes the key issues facing the women's institution after the creation of the BOP:

> After 1930 Alderson's relations to its superiors were characterized by continual conflict from which few areas were immune. In part, the struggle flowed from the bureau's push to consolidate its authority and to limit institutional autonomy. In part, it flowed from the fact that in many instances, the only point in the whole system where the [bureau] met any resistance was at [Alderson]. Most important, the men at the bureau disagreed with the women of Alderson's contention that as a women's institution it should be exempt from many policies and practices that had been devised for the largely male inmate population of the system. Whereas Alderson's correctional superiors in the 1920s included a powerful woman, Willebrandt, who agreed with the women-oriented approach, leadership of the Bureau of Prisons during the 1930s was composed of men who did not. Conflict was inevitable.

Women and BOP Policies

Ironically, the women-oriented approach of Alderson—a classification system, specialized programs for drug addiction, forms of inmate self-government, unit management, and cottage-style open institutions—became the pride of the BOP, but only when they became bureau policy and were instituted in men's institutions. The early introduction of classification boards in the bureau provides an interesting example of the process (Herschberger 1979).

In *Federal Offenders 1933-34*, Warden Hill of Lewisburg Penitentiary proudly reports that "this is possibly the only prison in the United States where every offender who has ever entered it has been required to appear before a board." Superintendent Harris (who fought the title of warden until 1937), in her section of the report, notes that at Alderson, where this had been the practice since the opening of the institution, not only does each new inmate come before the board, but every woman in the institution is reviewed every three months. In *Federal Offenders 1935-36*, Harris says that Alderson's classification process shaped its activities to conform with the general classification program of the department.

Interestingly, regarding those aspects of Alderson that were truly women-oriented—the cottage-centered kitchens and the presence of a nursery—Harris was either relatively silent or somewhat defensive. In *Federal Offenders 1930-31* she commented:

> A few years ago, there was a sentimental outcry against dooming the inmates of correctional institutions to the drudgery of the kitchen and of domestic service. My experience here and in other institutions has been that most women are greatful [sic] for the opportunity to learn how to keep house well.

She concluded by noting there is a good defense for training women *and men* in basic household skills.

In her regular reports in *Federal Offenders* from 1930 to 1940, there is no direct mention of the nursery at Alderson and only an occasional reference to the number of births to inmates, three in 1940 and a birth of triplets in May 1937. Nor do her memoirs touch this dimension of Alderson's programs. However, Lekkerkerker's (1931) description of Alderson includes mention of a "fine maternity cottage."

But only in later BOP descriptions of Alderson (1942 and 1957) is it noted that infant and child care classes become integral to the perception of Alderson as a women's institution. Prior to that (according to Virginia McLaughlin, Alderson's fifth female warden) in the late 1940s, Helen Hironimus, Alderson's second warden, accompanied her annual reports with pictures of babies to remind the central office that the babies were uncounted inmates, lost in the cost accounting of the bureau. Flynn (1963), in her inmate's view of Alderson in the 1950s, says the babies remained in the cottages with their mothers for a few months, and the parting of mother and child, especially if she faced a long sentence, was heartrending.

In the 1960s, federal judges were surprised at the number of babies born at Alderson, but were concerned that a difficult pregnancy might mean a fifty-mile trip on mountain highways to the nearest specialized hospital. But according to Virginia McLaughlin, the end of the era came when two social workers from the Department of Health, Education and Welfare visited and declared that "prison is no place for a child." Between the forces of centralization in the BOP that had difficulty handling a women's institution and a child-saving perspective from the social workers, Alderson lost its babies.

While Bates (1936) described Harris's administration as one of the federal correctional system's outstanding accomplishments, Bennett (1970), characterized Harris's tenure as one whose aim was to make Alderson replicate an "old-fashioned girls' school." Bennett credited himself with the creation of women's open institutions and experimentation in self-government. Alderson's remote location was viewed by him as the factor preventing a realistic rehabilitation program for women.

Changes in Security Levels

Significantly, Harris's efforts to demonstrate that women were as capable as men left her vulnerable to Bates's and Bennett's argument that female inmates should be treated like male inmates. The issue was exemplified in the conflict over whether there was a need for a maximum security federal facility for women. Harris's (1936) description of Alderson's "five rooms of reinforced concrete in the reception center and two small barred cottages for a possible forty-eight medium security women," with accompanying anecdotes on her handling of "resisters and smashers" and "molls," was in reaction to Bates' decision in 1933 (U.S. BOP 1933-34):

> The conviction of a number of women during the past year for serious and desperate crimes or for aiding gangsters and racketeers has made it necessary to provide a special place for their incarceration in an institution of the maximum security type. The Federal Industrial Institution for Women at Alderson was not designed and is not equipped to handle women who are desperate and incorrigible.

Harris argued that with inmate cooperation and skillful handling by staff, Alderson's open institution could handle all commitments. She denied the need for a separate facility for desperate and incorrigible women. Nevertheless, as Bates (1936) describes, at the newly opened Federal Detention Farm in Milan, Michigan, a small section of the cellblock was completely sealed off from the rest of the institution with twenty-two cells for women. In *Federal Offenders 1933-34*, Bates says the women would be adequately guarded by armed officers and housed in more traditional steel cells with a matron and a number of warders assisting the superintendent in guarding them.

In the intervening years, as reported by the detention farm's warden in *Federal Offenders 1940*, besides housing problem women, the institution housed informers, narcotic addicts, psychopaths, and homosexuals. In 1936, a transition year from Bates's administration to Bennett's, Bennett called for a maximum security institution for women: "We need to specialize our institutions for women just as we have done for men." Citing the fact that Alderson was crowded, with more than 200 women boarded out at nonfederal institutions under contract, he said a new jail was planned for Terminal Island in California that would accommodate 24 women in a wing of a facility built to house 600 men. Despite his call for specialization, the new maximum security institution as Bennett described it would house

> ...not only the approximately 250 women who come from western districts at a considerable saving in transportation costs but also accept those most difficult cases originating in other sections of the country... unregenerate keepers of houses of prostitution, gangsters, molls, and confirmed drug users.

Harris fought back. In her superintendent's report she responded:

> It seems that the time has come, which was anticipated when this

institution was built, to plan for an institution west of the Mississippi, built like this on the cottage plan...to care for a population of 500, and with cottage facilities for 300 at the outset.

The issue was one of principle:

I do not believe that a maximum security institution for women is necessary, and I feel that it would be a decided letting down of our standard if such an institution were proposed. I am convinced that we have made a demonstration here which has set a standard for the country and that it would be considered a setback if we should depart from the policy so far adopted here and in well-conducted state institutions for women.

However, her argument was weakened by her request that the courts select cases for Alderson in which there was the greatest possibility of "reclamation." By implication, the other women would be contracted to the states.

In 1938, Bennett approached the House Appropriations Committee with a request for three new institutions—one a women's facility in the Southwest: "It is an extremely expensive and undesirable situation to be forced to transport these women all the way to Alderson." In 1937, more than 1,267 federal female offenders had been committed from the courts, with 400 sent to Alderson and the rest to state institutions.

A congressman asked Bennett whether the new women's institution he was planning to build would be similar to Alderson. Bennett said it would be more in line with a maximum security institution. Twenty-five long-term problem female inmates and the drug-addict population would be taken out of Milan and divided between Alderson and the new institution. Bennett admitted that "certain women's organizations feel we are discriminating against female offenders because there are no facilities [comparable with the facilities at Lexington and Fort Worth] for handling female addicts."

The new Federal Reformatory for Women officially opened on 10 October 1940 in Seagoville, Texas, with a capacity for 400 women. But it was an open institution, situated on farmland and built on a cottage plan similar to that of Alderson. It appears that Harris won and Bennett lost. How did it happen?

The records are scanty. A 1958 brochure on Seagoville indicated that the first warden, Helen Hironimus, (Harris's long-time friend and assistant) "good-naturedly begged, cajoled, and browbeat her Washington superiors into giving her funds for the progressive development of its plant." However, it appears that the coalition of progressive women's clubs that helped bring Alderson into being may have been rallied again. In *Federal Offenders 1936-1937*, Harris described the tenth anniversary celebration in May 1937 of Alderson's founding. Key participants in the earlier victory, Mabel Walker Willebrandt and Julia K. Jaffrey, as well as the chair of the Public Welfare Committee of the General Federation of Women's Clubs, gave speeches. Bennett was present. In other reports, Harris describes Eleanor Roosevelt's visits and interest in Alderson. There is some indication from the nature of the questions at House Appropriation hearings that the women's clubs had significantly affected members of the Appropriations Committees as well as the director of the BOP.

By 1941, when 104 women were at Seagoville, the members of the House Appropriations Committee quizzed Bennett on a $5,000 item for fencing: Was it to keep cattle or people in? Bennett replied that it was to keep cattle in and people out. The congressmen appeared somewhat startled to discover that the women were doing the farming: "But they drive the tractors?...They bring home the cows and do all the regular farm work?" Bennett replied affirmatively.

World War II and After

The history of Seagoville as a women's institution was short-lived. In 1941, with the retirement of Mary Belle Harris, Helen Hironimus returned to Alderson as warden. Amy N. Stannard, who had been a member of the bureau's first parole board, moved from assistant to warden. In March 1942, Seagoville became a Federal Detention Station for Japanese, German, and Italian families. Amy Stannard remained as administrator, but the female staff and inmates returned to Alderson.

In 1940 Bennett reported to the members of the House Appropriations Committee that Milan's notorious cases had been transferred to Terminal Island (a men's facility that had a wing for women). The removal of the women from Milan brought the number of women at Terminal Island to fifty-six. According to the warden's report in *Federal Offenders 1940*, while vocational training for men was limited, vocational training for women was "progressing nicely," with all of the female inmates enrolled in one or more of the following: music, sewing, knitting, dressmaking, weaving, nursing, and laundry work.

The next year at the appropriation hearings, a congressman raised the question: "What was the reason for having women at Terminal Island? Was there any effort to move them to any other place?" Bennett responded: "Yes, sir. We are moving these women to Dallas. We put them at Terminal Island simply because we had no other place to put them." Due to World War II, Terminal Island closed along with Seagoville in 1942. Some of the women were put in nonfederal institutions, while others joined the women at Alderson.

Fifteen years after its founding, Alderson was once again the only federal institution for female offenders. Ironically, during World War II, it performed the function that during World War I transformed former brothels into federal detention centers for women. With the passage of the May Act, patterned after the World War I antivice legislation, Alderson became the temporary home for several hundred women arrested for prostitution in military areas. In 1945, it was reported that 52 percent of the women committed to Alderson that year suffered from venereal disease (BOP 1945-59). Perhaps the situation can best be described as providing a final twist to an end of an era for women in federal corrections.

In the years after 1945, as earlier in its history, changes occurring in the larger society affected both the bureau and Alderson. After the Supreme Court decision on school desegregation, Alderson's racially segregated cottages were integrated by 1956. Terminal Island reopened in 1955, and women again occupied a section of the prison. The resurgence of the women's movement, with demands for equal treatment, combined with increasing numbers of female inmates, brought co-corrections to the BOP in the 1970s. Appropriately, it first occurred in the very institutions—Fort Worth and Lexington—that, as drug treatment centers, the earlier women's organizations had complained were not open to women. Like segregated school systems, where separate but equal programs are seldom achieved, the move to integrate corrections for women provided a range of educational and occupational choices historically limited in women's institutions by funding and size.

Alderson, however, remained the women's institution, although a slow recognition in the 1950s that female correctional officers were equally entitled to a forty-hour work week had brought an end to the family-style cottages with kitchens and resident officers. While Title VII of the Civil Rights Act brought changes in the litigation and investigations of prison conditions for female offenders at the state and federal level in the context of the equal protection clause brought visibility to women's prisons. The U.S. Commission on Civil Rights investigated Alderson in 1974, while the West Virginia Advisory Committee voiced their concerns over the human and civil rights of Alderson's inmates and their unique problems as women.

With the retirement in 1976 of Virginia McLaughlin, Alderson's new warden was a man. Mary Belle Harris' belief that it was essential for a woman to be in charge no longer was a reality.

In the 1990s Alderson remains a women's institution, but no longer in its historic role as the central facility for women. It is now a camp in the hills of West Virginia, serving minimum security women. Twelve other facilities, including a maximum security wing at the Federal Correctional Institution in Marianna, Florida, house the approximately five thousand women under bureau custody. At the same time, women serve at every level of the BOP. In the footsteps of Mabel Willebrandt and Mary Belle Harris, women are moving up career ladders to head men's as well as women's institutions. But the concerns that Mabel Willebrandt and Mary Belle Harris raised as women in the 1920s are still with us.

References

Bates, Sanford. 1936. *Prisons and beyond.* New York: Macmillan.

Bennett, James V. 1970. *I chose prison.* New York: Knopf.

Brown, Dorothy M. 1984. *Mabel Walker Willebrandt: A study of power, loyalty, and law.* Knoxville, Tenn.: University of Tennessee Press.

Flynn, Elizabeth G. 1963. *The Alderson story: My life as a political prisoner.* New York: International Publishers.

Harris, Mary B. 1936. *I knew them in prison.* New York: Viking.

Hershberger, Gregory L. 1979. *The development of the federal prison system.* Marion, Ill.: UNICOR.

Lekkerkerker, Eugenia C. 1931. *Reformatories for women in the United States.* Batavia, The Netherlands: J. B. Wolters.

SchWeber, Claudine. 1982. The government's unique experiment in salvaging women criminals: Cooperation and conflict in the administration of a women's prison—the case of the Federal Industrial Institution for Women at Alderson. In *Judge, lawyer, victim, thief: Women, gender roles and criminal justice*, ed. Nicole H. Rafter and Elizabeth A. Stanko. Boston: Northeastern University.

U.S. Bureau of Prisons. 1930-1945. Federal offenders. Leavenworth, Kans.: Federal Industries Press.

U.S. Bureau of Prisons. 1945-1959. Federal Prisons. Leavenworth, Kans.: Federal Industries Press.

V.

From Victim to Victimizer

by Crista Brett, Psy.D.

While journalists chronicle acts of violence on an unprecedented scale—in our homes and on our city streets—the criminal justice system struggles with an ever-increasing number of inmates, raising concern about the increasing potential for violence in law enforcement and correctional settings.

Many inmates have been victims of violence, before and during their victimization of others. Understanding the violence cycle in families helps us deal more effectively with the mental health and socialization needs of inmates. Addressing the cycle of victimization is especially important when it comes to women.

Women and Abuse

In early 1991, a number of Federal Bureau of Prisons officials who work with women came together to discuss issues affecting the female offender. One important issue was the effect of abuse on women. It has been suggested that, worldwide, more women and children are killed or injured every year as a result of domestic violence than any other cause (such as disease, accident, or war). Recent statistics demonstrate that reported cases of serious child abuse have increased by 35 percent, and death from child abuse has increased in many states (Hackett, McKillop & Wang 1988). It is estimated that America's police spend almost a third of their time responding to domestic violence calls (Freeman 1979).

Every eighteen seconds a woman is beaten in the United States. It is estimated that six out of every ten women have been abused at some point in their lives. Every year, about 4,000 women are killed due to domestic violence. One-third of all women who leave an abusive relationship will be assaulted again by their abusive partner (Kaufman & Zigler 1987). Many female inmates have been victims of domestic abuse as adults and have witnessed spousal abuse as children. In one study of children who murder, more than 75 percent had been exposed to violence and abuse, especially sexual abuse during childhood (Lewis et al. 1985). Child abuse and neglect are thought to be on the increase due to drug abuse (Hackett, McKillop & Wang 1988). Drug abuse by parental figures is likewise thought to be a factor in the disinhibition of violence in the family and neglectful

Crista Brett, Psy. D., formerly employee assistance program coordinator for the Federal Bureau of Prisons, now works for Indian Health Services as the director of behavioral health at the Wind River Reservation in Ft. Washaskie, Wyoming.

behavior (Gropper 1984). For every reported case of child abuse, it is estimated that as many as ten go unreported (Wolock & Horowitz 1984).

Many inmates have experienced abuse in their lives. In a study of female inmates who were given prison terms for killing their children, each had a history of severe rejection, neglect, or abuse. Many inmates with a history of severe alcohol abuse reported receiving little parental affection and remember being seriously punished. They also reported severe parental conflict in their families of origin (Gayford 1975).

Some of the psychological effects of long-term spousal and child abuse are similar to the effects of being taken hostage. A very strong bond is created between victim and victimizer—so strong that hostages have tried to stay with their captors after the terms of release have been negotiated, and abused children and wives have lied about their injuries to protect their abusers (Dutton & Painter 1981). Researchers have suggested that memories of a traumatic situation are ingrained more deeply and affect behavior more directly than memories developed under normal circumstances. This may help explain the strength of a victim's emotional response—even though it seemingly defies logic. This bond has been labeled the ''Stockholm syndrome'' in hostage events and ''traumatic bonding'' when discussing spousal or child abuse (Dutton & Painter 1981).

The Cycle of Violence

Walker (1980) has described a cycle of violence in families—a tension-building phase, an explosive battering phase, and a calm and loving phase that some call the ''honeymoon phase.'' An abuser tends to give intermittent reinforcement to the victim. Sometimes the abuser may be kind and rewarding to the victim and at other times may attack. (A positive reward may be something as simple as allowing the victim to live.)

This system of reward and punishment is similar to the experience of gambling. Slot machines use the principle of intermittent reinforcement. For example, when a person pulls a slot machine's arm, he or she is either rewarded with money or punished with no money. People can develop all kinds of ideas about this process. They may believe that a certain slot machine is lucky or ''hot,'' that a reward will surely come on a specific time or day, or that God will grant them the money for good behavior. These belief systems help people convince themselves that they are in control of a chance phenomenon, even though they aren't. Once the behavior is learned, it is difficult to extinguish—the chance of winning is always there. If they don't win on the first or second pull, maybe they will on the fifteenth.

Women in a battering relationship attempt to keep it in the honeymoon phase, behaving in ways that will be rewarded and avoiding behavior that will be punished. Many times, however, the punishments and rewards are not linked to behavior, even though the victim may choose to believe they are. Victims may develop inferences about the abuser's behavior in an attempt to feel in control. These inferences can have magical or superstitious qualities and have little to do with the abuser's actual behavior. Many victims work to read every mood of the victimizer in an attempt to avert punishment. Women and children who have been abused tend to be acutely aware of other people's thoughts and feelings and unaware of their own thoughts and feelings. They have learned over time that survival depends on pleasing others. When an individual is victimized, she begins to lose any sense of self-efficacy in the abusive situation. This loss carries over to other situations. Many abused women believe they are helpless to escape or unworthy of escaping and think they have no value to other people (Dutton & Painter 1981). Some believe that their faults cause the abuse, not the abuser's faults.

Reliving Victimization

Traumatic events can be reenacted in many ways. Individuals may experience nightmares and intrusive memories of the traumatic event. They may avoid places, events, or people who remind them of a traumatic occurrence. People may also deliberately reenact traumas in an attempt to master them; such reenactments can take the form of harm to others, harm to self, or revictimization. For example, if a man was sexually molested as a young boy, he may sexually molest other young boys when he reaches maturity. In this way, he gains control over a frightening event by being the perpetrator instead of the victim (Van der Kolk 1989).

Rape victims have been known to walk in dangerous parts of town in an attempt to be involved in another attack. They unconsciously hope to prevail in this attack so they won't continue to feel victimized. Women who have been victims of violence tend to reenact their abuse as victims; men who were victims tend to reenact their abuse as victimizers. Many prostitutes have histories of sexual molestation as children, and prostitution appears to be a behavioral reenactment of that molestation. Unfortunately, the woman is never able to master the trauma, and it repeats itself over and over.

Van der Kolk (1989) described some physiological changes that can occur in victims of trauma. When a woman has been traumatized, she tends to experience chronic physiological hyperarousal. Behaviorally, victims demonstrate deficits in learning novel behavior, may experience chronic subjective stress, and may have increased tumor genesis and immunosuppression. Chemicals in the brain, such as serotonin, norepinephrine, and endorphins, may be unbalanced as a result of hyperarousal.

Research with animals and humans has shown that when an organism is overly aroused it will persevere in familiar behavior even when the familiar is self-destructive. If you put an animal in a cage with no means of escape and shock it, it will probably cower in a corner. If you repeat this procedure numerous times, then open the cage door, chances are the animal will remain in the corner. This unwillingness to attempt new behavior has been labeled "learned helplessness." It is easy to see how, when a person has lived in a situation of chronic abuse, the motivation to avoid rearousing conflict may become so great that she will choose a course of action without thinking through the consequences.

Hyperarousal can also have a paradoxical effect. Occasionally people (and animals too) will become addicted to stress and seek greater and greater levels of stress to obtain release. High levels of stress tend to activate natural opoids called endorphins—probably most familiar as the substance causing the so-called "runners' high." Once a person has adapted to one level of stress, she or he must seek a greater level of stress to get the same endorphin high. This theory has been applied to people who self-mutilate, using the reasoning that mutilating one's body increases the level of stress, and endorphins would thus be released. To test this theory, researchers blocked the opoid receptors in the brains of subjects. The result was a reduction in mutilation attempts (Van der Kolk 1989).

The Challenge for Correctional Workers

People who have been victimized tend to view the world pessimistically. Traumatic bonding is an extremely powerful bond and highly resistant to change. Abused women often do not have the same freedom or capacity for problem solving and decision making as women who have never been abused.

Education and therapy are proven tools in the care of traumatic stress reactions. It is important to help abused female inmates work through the traumatic content of their lives and explore the ways in which they have constricted their thinking and behavior. Staff will need to address issues of suicidal ideation and behavior, revictimization, and intentional harm to others. Many victims believe that the type of attachment behavior they have experienced—the only type of bonding to which they have been exposed—is love. They need to be given the tools to form less violent, more stable relationships in the future.

Working with inmates who have family histories of abuse is paramount because they will be the caretakers of the next generation. Victims need to be educated about the effects of violence on their offspring; they cannot be expected to be good parents without the proper tools. Many of these women have never had proper child care models. The type of parenting they have seen and experienced is often extremely destructive.

Many victims have learned that violent confrontation is the way to win an argument. They need to be given skills to solve confrontation without violence. It would also be helpful to educate women about chronic hyperarousal and give them tools such as biofeedback to monitor their progress. Ultimately, they must come to understand what constitutes a healthy relationship, rather than simply moving from one battering relationship to another.

The choices we make now in corrections will affect the coming generations. It would be good to know that knowledge about the effects of domestic violence was put to work and that those who work with female inmates may have contributed to a few more children and a few more women achieving stable, loving relationships.

References

Dutton, D., and S. L. Painter. 1981. Traumatic bonding: The development of emotional attachments in battered women and other relationships of intermittent abuse. *Victimology* 6:139-55.

Freeman, M. D. 1979. *Violence in the home*. Farnborough, England: Saxon House.

Gayford, J. 1975. Wife-battering: A preliminary study of 100 cases. *British Journal of Medicine* 15:243-44.

Gropper, B. A. 1984. Probing the links between drugs and crime. *NIJ Reports* (November): 4-8.

Hackett, G., P. McKillop, and D. Wang. 1988. A tale of abuse: The Steinberg trial. *Newsweek* (12 December): 56-8.

Kaufman, J., and E. Zigler. 1987. Do abused children become abusive parents? *American Journal of Orthopsychiatry* 57(2):186-91.

Lewis, D., et al. 1985. Biopsychosocial characteristics of children who later murder: A prospective study. *American Journal of Psychiatry* 142(10):1161-67.

Van der Kolk, B. 1989. The trauma spectrum: The interaction of biological and social events in the genesis of the trauma response. *Journal of Traumatic Stress Studies* 1:273-90.

Walker, L. E. 1980. *The battered woman*. New York: HarperCollins Publisher

Wolock, I., and B. Horowitz. 1984. Child maltreatment as a social problem: The neglect of neglect. *American Journal of Orthopsychiatry* 54:530-41.

VI.

Legal Issues and the Female Offender

by Marjorie Van Ochten, J.D.

Legal issues and litigation by inmates are of concern to correctional administrators. Although this was not always the case, it has been the reality for the past several years, at least since the mid-1970s when the federal courts began issuing a number of decisions that outlined inmates' rights and substantially affected the way correctional administrators conduct their business.

All of the legal concerns that affect male inmates, of course, apply equally to female inmates, such as access to the courts, the practice of religion, and receiving publications through the mail. However, although most of the lawsuits that outlined these rights, if not all, were brought by male inmates, there are some areas of litigation and legal issues that are primarily of concern in dealing with female inmates. This chapter will attempt to summarize the principle areas of litigation by female inmates to give correctional administrators an understanding and perhaps a starting point for further exploration to avoid litigation.

The Issue of Parity

In prisons, the doctrine of "separate but equal" is permissible. Male and female inmates can be, and often are, housed in separate institutions. The problem for most states has been there are so few female inmates relative to the number of male inmates that equality in programming and other areas has been difficult to achieve. In addition to cost concerns and other problems, the day-to-day crises of the 95 percent or more of the population that is male are often so overwhelming that the 5 percent or less of the population that is female gets neglected. This can be a very costly mistake.

Michigan has struggled with this issue since a federal judge ruled in 1979 that the state was not providing equal programming for its female inmates. The case in which this ruling was made, which has been referred to as the "leading case" in this area, is *Glover v. Johnson* (478 F. Supp. 1075 [1979]). In this class-action lawsuit, it was claimed that the Department of Corrections had denied its female

Marjorie Van Ochten, J. D., is the administrator of the Office of Policy and Hearings for the Michigan Department of Corrections.

inmates their constitutional right to due process and equal protection by offering educational and vocational rehabilitation opportunities substantially inferior to those provided to male inmates.

The department argued that its women's prison (at the time there was only one) offered programming that was at least comparable, if not better, than what was offered at a similarly sized male facility. The judge, however, cited the fact that while male inmates could be sent to a variety of prisons and thus had access to programming at all of these facilities, female inmates had only one place to go and thus were limited to the programming offered at that single facility. The judge decided that equal protection required parity of treatment, as contrasted with identical treatment, to provide female inmates with the same access to rehabilitation opportunities that were being provided to male inmates.

The final order in *Glover* was not issued until 1981, after more than a year of negotiations between the parties as to its terms, and covered a wide range of issues (*Glover v. Johnson*, 510 F. Supp. 1019 [1981]). The department was ordered to provide two-year college programming, enhanced vocational offerings, apprenticeship opportunities, and prison industries, which had previously existed only at men's institutions. The court also ordered paralegal training and access to attorneys to remedy past inadequacies in law library facilities. It required the department to redo its inmate wage policy to ensure that female inmates were provided equal wages and ordered that a minimum security camp for females be provided to permit female inmates to have access to the unique programming that was provided at camps that had previously been available only for men.

In the area of vocational programming, the court was particularly concerned about what it found to be the inferior quality and types of programs offered to the women, as well as the fact that fewer programs were offered. For example, the judge cited the food service program at the women's facility, which was geared to noncommercial short order cooking skills, while the program at a men's prison focused on commercial cooking. The judge was clearly troubled by sexual stereotyping in the types and quality of programming offered, as has been reinforced several times in subsequent years as the department has struggled to comply with the court's directives. There has been a continual emphasis on "nontraditional" programming for women, such as providing vocational courses in automotive maintenance and carpentry.

The *Glover* case is an ongoing concern of the Michigan Department of Corrections. The state has been involved in two lengthy contempt proceedings and two appeals to the U.S. Court of Appeals for the Sixth Circuit. In 1991, the department hired a special administrator, at the order of the court, to design and implement a plan to bring the department into compliance with the orders in *Glover*.

The lesson to be learned from Michigan's experience is to provide programming and other opportunities to female inmates at a level that will withstand court scrutiny to avoid having to develop and implement these programs under a court's watchful eyes.

Several other states have been faced with litigation regarding the issue of parity of female programming, although such cases are often settled by consent judgments. According to Nicole Hahn Rafter (1990), a professor of criminal justice at Northeastern University:

> The majority of these cases do not go to trial. Sometimes the mere threat

of litigation forces states to take action. On other occasions, state and inmates reach an agreement that avoids trial.

She cites cases in Connecticut, California, Wisconsin, and Idaho, all of which have been settled without trial. Other states have litigated such claims with limited success. (See *McCoy v. Nevada Department of Prisons*, 776 F. Supp. 521 [1991].) In *McCoy* the court again emphasized the heightened standard of review for claims of unequal treatment based on sex and clearly stated that only important government objectives could justify unequal treatment.

If a state believes that it has achieved parity and equal treatment for female inmates based on the above standard but is still faced with litigation, it can take heart from a decision of the Sixth Circuit Court of Appeals involving claims by female inmates in Kentucky that their rights had been violated. In 1989, in the case of *Canterino v. Wilson* (869 F. 2d 948), the court of appeals reversed the lower court and ruled that the inmates had failed to prove their allegations of discrimination. Thus, claims of unequal treatment are not always successful.

The Right to Privacy

While parity and equal treatment in programming and conditions of incarceration are clearly the major legal issues that should concern correctional administrators when dealing with female inmates, it is not the only issue that has been litigated. An emphasis on equal employment opportunity, as well as other factors, has increased the use of male correctional officers in women's prisons. This has, in turn, created litigation involving the alleged violation of female inmates' right to privacy by the assigning of male officers to housing units and subjecting female inmates to searches done by male officers.

In an early case in this area, a federal court in New York ruled that male officers could not be assigned to the night shift in a housing unit where they might see a female inmate unclothed or using the toilet during their rounds. However, the court upheld the assignment of male officers to daytime duties where adequate accommodations could be made to achieve a balance between the inmates' right to privacy and the state's need to maintain order and security in the prison. For example, by the use of modesty panels in shower areas. However, the Court of Appeals for the Second Circuit overturned the lower court on the issue of night assignments and ruled that male correctional officers could perform such duty as long as proper sleepwear was provided to the female inmates. (See *Forts v. Ward*, 621 F. 2d 1210 [1980].)

Most of the court cases in which inmates have argued that their right to privacy has been violated have involved complaints by male inmates about female officers. Almost all of these cases have also been unsuccessful in establishing a violation of inmates' rights. This makes all the more surprising a 1988 decision by the Court of Appeals for the Seventh Circuit in the case of *Torres v. Wisconsin Department of Health and Social Services* (854 F. 2d 1523) where the court upheld a ban on male officers being assigned to the housing units in a female facility. However, privacy interests were not the basis for this decision, and in fact, the court rejected that claim. The winning argument for the State of Wisconsin was that the assignment of male officers to women's housing units would impede rehabilitation efforts of female offenders due to the large percentage of them who had been physically and sexually abused by males. Although the U.S. Supreme Court declined to hear an appeal of this decision, it is questionable how much weight the decision would be given in other circuits in light of the overwhelming number of decisions that have been found in favor of equal employment opportunity for both male and female officers rather than inmates' rights.

The other area where the rights of female inmates and male officers clash is in the performance of patdown and strip searches. As with challenges to housing assignments, most search cases have been brought by male inmates objecting to searches done by female staff. In one case brought by female inmates was *Jordan v. Gardner* (953 F. 2d 1137 [1992]). The case involved routine pat searches of female inmates by male correctional officers. The U.S. Court of Appeals for the 9th Circuit reversed a lower court decision and held that such searches did not violate the inmates' rights. The lower court had found persuasive the argument that differing treatment of women in free society caused greater concern for female inmates who were pat searched by males than was the case for male inmates being searched by female officers. While this argument may well have some basis in fact, the court of appeals was not convinced that the impact was significant enough to justify a different result than had been their holding in earlier decisions where they had upheld searches of male inmates by female officers. The results in this case reinforce the belief that the *Torres* case may be an aberration.

The issue of male officers conducting routine strip searches of female inmates has not been litigated, probably because few correctional administrators would permit such a practice both for practical reasons and due to the court decisions involving male inmates and female staff, which clearly seem to limit such searches to nonroutine or emergency situations. In one reported case involving a female inmate, *Lee v. Downs* (641 F. 2d 1117 [1981]), the Court of Appeals for the Fourth Circuit upheld the use of male officers during the strip search of a female inmate due to the emergency nature of the situation. Judging from this case, the same standards of emergency would seem to apply in strip searches of female inmates with male staff involved as has been the case for male inmates with female staff involved.

In many of these search cases, the issue of the professionalism of staff is a central concern. If male officers are being allowed to pat search female inmates it is clearly advisable to ensure that proper training is provided and that professional standards are carefully enforced.

Sexual Contact

The issues raised by the question of searches also surface in another area where courts have become involved in the subject of the interactions between female inmates and male staff. That area is sexual contact between staff and inmates, including claims of sexual assault. Michigan is not unique in having had such litigation brought by female inmates. These issues surface wherever there is cross-gender supervision, and even where there is same-sex supervision. But clearly the undercurrent of the cases involving searching and housing assignments, if not the clear arguments of plaintiffs in such cases, involves an acknowledgment that sexual harassment and assault of women by men is much more prevalent than the reverse. Correctional administrators attempting to integrate male staff into a female facility may find themselves faced with increasing legal activity in the form of prosecutions of staff for sexual assault as well as lawsuits by female inmates claiming a violation of their Eighth Amendment rights by failure to protect them from sexual assaults.

Clearly, care in the selection, training, and supervision of staff is essential in dealing with such claims and avoiding potential liability. Besides considerations of professionalism, an additional incentive for staff in the State of Michigan to avoid such sexual contact has been the enactment of a statute in 1988 that makes even consensual sexual contact with a inmate by an employee of the Department of Corrections a misdemeanor punishable by up to two years of imprisonment. Such a law makes arguments of "enticement" a moot issue.

Health Care Concerns

A final area where legal issues may be raised is that of health care services to female inmates. The same legal theories may be used as are used in parity cases, but they surface in a unique manner. Where there are medical concerns that affect only female inmates, such as pregnancy and childbirth, correctional administrators must be careful to ensure that they do not enact policies that treat these medical conditions differently than other conditions, both in terms of access to necessary treatment and eligibility for programming and work assignments.

The provision of mental health services is another area where states may be vulnerable. As with other programming, the small number of female inmates in proportion to the number of male inmates may raise problems of equal access to services. Many prison systems have a sufficient number of mentally ill male inmates to devote an entire hospital facility to their care. However, unless the facility is constructed to also permit the safe housing of mentally ill female inmates, they may not receive comparable care. Some states provide for such services through their state department of mental health or private contractors, but whatever is done, care must be taken to ensure that mentally ill female inmates receive the same services provided to mentally ill male inmates, even if the per capita cost of providing such services is greater for females.

Female Inmates and Litigation

If you are a correctional administrator, at this point you may be wondering why you have never been sued on any of these issues if they are indeed of such concern. The answer may lie in the fact that female inmates simply do not file lawsuits as often as male inmates. The experience in Michigan has certainly shown that to be the case.

Michigan officials recently took a look at the number of lawsuits filed by female inmates in 1988 and 1989. (These years were chosen because the subsequent years of 1990 and 1991 were complicated by the closure of women's prisons and movement of inmates to formerly male institutions.) Although women comprised approximately 5 percent of the prison population in 1988, they initiated only 1.5 percent of the lawsuits filed by inmates against the department that year. In 1989, when inmates filed a total of over 1,200 lawsuits against the department, less than 1 percent of those cases were filed by female inmates.

The reasons for this are not clear in that female inmates in Michigan have access to the same lawbooks as male inmates and have had that access for several years. They also have a comparable, if not higher, rate of literacy. In addition, due to the *Glover* case, they have been provided with paralegal training. Several theories have been put forth to explain this lesser inclination to litigate on the part of female inmates, such as their greater focus on other concerns like the well-being of their children, as well as the social conditioning of women, which makes them less likely to assert their rights.

Whatever the reasons may be, it is clear that the lack of litigation by female inmates is not due to a lack of issues to be litigated. Correctional administrators who have not yet been faced with these issues may do well to take the opportunity to remedy any problems they may have in the areas discussed to avoid costly and troublesome litigation.

Reference

Rafter, Nicole Hahn. 1990. Equal protection forcing changes in women's prisons. *Correctional Law* (September).

VII.

Tailoring Facility Programming to Suit Female Offenders' Needs

by Scarlett V. Carp and Linda S. Schade

The unique characteristics of female inmates—their roles as parents; their histories of abuse, dependency, and poor work skills; and their low education levels—need to be addressed through programming.

If the probability of recidivism is to be reduced, corrections agencies must provide programs that teach self-sufficiency, improved interpersonal relationships, and responsible behavior, among others. An agency's support for programming is reflected by its management approach and operating philosophy. Its concern for programming also can be incorporated into the design of new prisons.

Who Is the Female Offender?

Of the 823,414 inmates reportedly incarcerated in state and federal prisons at the end of 1991, women accounted for 47,691, or 5.8 percent, according to the Bureau of Justice Statistics (1988). About half of these women were sentenced for property crimes or robbery and about 20 percent were convicted of murder or manslaughter. The typical female offender is under thirty years old, African American, poorly educated, and unemployed or employed as a low-skilled worker. More than half of the women in prison have children.

A significant number of female offenders come from backgrounds of poverty, neglect, and abuse. They are likely to have histories of emotional problems linked with drug or alcohol abuse. Their physical health is generally poor. Consequently, they often arrive in prison frightened, ill, and unable to cope with the circumstances confronting them.

One of the female offender's most urgent concerns is her children. Although some children live with a relative while their mother is in prison, as many as one

Scarlett V. Carp is president of Scarlett Carp and Associates Inc., a planning and management consultant firm with offices in Washington, D.C., and Sacramento, Calif.

Linda S. Schade is a planning associate with the firm's California office.

child in eight is placed in foster care. Offenders often worry about the loss of parental rights, which are sometimes terminated because mothers are judged unfit due to their incarceration. Efforts made to keep mothers and children together and to ensure contact in prison and a healthy environment on release vary widely from state to state.

Problems of Incarceration

Women adapt to prison differently than men and are much less likely to engage in violence during incarceration. Instead, they seek to recreate or establish the kinds of relationships they are most familiar with: family bonds. Women are much more likely than men to maintain regular family contact by visit, phone, or mail.

The female offender usually arrives in prison with a long history of unmet needs, perhaps the most crucial of which is the need for independence. She wants to gain economic independence by acquiring better job skills, and she admires women who can take care of themselves. Unfortunately, the system in which she is incarcerated very often discourages her from attaining that goal.

Feihman (1983) has written about how the prison environment and recent theories of female criminality reinforce the traditional female roles of wife, mother, and homemaker. She points out that most vocational programs available to female inmates concentrate on low-paying occupations consistent with this traditional concept, such as sewing, cleaning, food service, and cosmetology.

Given that the majority of available training programs emphasize traditional female occupations, inmates are likely to find it difficult to escape reinforcement of the idea that they should be a homemaker or low-skilled worker. Female inmates often receive the same kind of job training that led to them being underemployed or unemployed in the first place, and their educational deficits are left unaddressed. The culture of a women's prison often supports this traditional dependent role. The tightly structured prison environment deprives women of control over basic decisions such as where they will be and with whom, what and when they will eat, and how their days will be structured.

Moreover, prisons typically do not prepare inmates to face the challenges of returning to the outside world. Issues confronting the paroled inmate include whether her skills will enable her to find a job, the adequacy of low wages she is likely to be paid, and the care of her children while she is at work. These issues often go unaddressed in correctional programming for women, reinforcing the notion that women can find someone to take care of them.

Ways to Improve Programming

A prison administrator's management style significantly influences the facility's character and atmosphere, inmate behavior, and staff and inmate perceptions. A unit management approach promotes the development of mutually beneficial relationships between staff and inmates. This approach places line staff and mid-level managers in daily contact with the inmates and allows staff of all disciplines (supervisors, officers, counselors, educators, clinicians, case managers, etc.) to work closely with each other, fostering a positive, caring, and efficient working relationship.

Programming should show inmates they have control of their future and offer practical opportunities to develop literacy, vocational, parenting, and social skills. Counseling and treatment should be available to address problems associated with substance abuse, emotional disturbances, self-confidence, and self-esteem. Inmates should proceed through a series of phases that take them logically from one skill level to the next, building on the skills gained in each previous phase. These phases span an inmate's entire incarceration period, from assessment and diagnosis through work release and parole.

Assessment and Diagnosis

The first phase of the delivery system begins at intake. Ideally, newly admitted offenders should be housed in a diagnostic unit and administered a battery of social, psychological, academic, and vocational aptitude tests. A medical evaluation is extremely important to determine whether an inmate is a substance abuser and to identify visual or auditory deficiencies that may impede her ability to learn.

From these and other assessments, a comprehensive profile can be assembled for each inmate. This is then used for classification and the development of the inmate's program plan.

Most jurisdictions require new inmates to attend orientation sessions to familiarize them with the prison's philosophy, operations, rules and regulations, and available services and programs. This time can also be used to emphasize the expectation that they will participate in programs while incarcerated.

Housing Assignments

Housing assignments should be based on the information gathered in the first phase. Inmates who show they are motivated can be assigned together to reinforce positive goal attainment. Conversely, women who demonstrate predatory or acting-out behavior should be housed separately from those who respond more positively.

Work and Training Assignments

Work and training assignments are a critical phase of a female inmate's incarceration. To be effective, an inmate's program plan should address her academic deficiencies first and then give her practical skills through meaningful vocational and prison industries assignments.

Literacy skills, for example, are crucial to success in vocational programs that require reading technical manuals. Reading and writing skills also are essential to an inmate's ability to get a job and live an independent life in the outside world. The degree to which work and vocational programs emphasize skills and occupations not traditionally taught to women, such as electronics, computer programming, and carpentry, is a critical factor in determining an inmate's successful transition to the community.

It is also important that vocational and industries programs teach and provide skills for which there is a demand in the job market. Public and private partnerships in prison industries that provide training and the opportunity to continue employment with the company when the inmate is released are, obviously, the most desirable.

Special Needs Programming

Programming to address emotional disturbance and substance abuse is a critical part of the female offender's overall program plan. Staff responsible for program planning should be encouraged to work closely with mental health and substance abuse clinicians to ensure an integrated approach to addressing an inmate's special needs.

Mental health services and programs should range from assessment to individual and group counseling to crisis care to dedicated residential treatment units supervised by cross-trained staff. Transfers to inpatient hospital psychiatric care must be available for those who require it. Transition services to community resources are needed for inmates' return to the community.

Programming for substance abuse should include self-help groups, such as Alcoholics Anonymous and Narcotics Anonymous, education and counseling programs for general population inmates, and residential programs with intensive transitional treatment programming for inmates who are soon to be paroled.

Intensive transitional treatment programs for the highly motivated should include a structured program that takes place within the context of a therapeutic community. In addition, referrals to postcustody services are essential to the inmate's successful reentry into the community and her ability to remain drug-free.

Socialization Programs

A key to the problem of inmates' low self-esteem is the way they view themselves in the context of their social and family environment. Socialization programs provide a strong vehicle for teaching female inmates new values pertinent to their roles as women.

Socialization programs include special programs to address self-esteem, life skills, parenting, and job readiness. Self-esteem programs target the woman's view of herself in all areas of her life, including her relationships with men. The fact that physical, sexual, and mental abuse has characterized these relationships does little to change her ability to break this self-destructive cycle.

Mentoring relationships with people from the community, special groups that focus on resolving issues of abuse, and other special purpose programs encourage women to actively take control of their lives.

Life skills training encompasses a number of areas, including career planning, continuing education, employment application and interviewing, finding adequate housing and child care, budgeting and household management, banking, and buying on credit.

Family programs offer a variety of options for mothers and their children, including overnight visits, day visits, holiday and special occasion programs, and parenting classes. Parenting classes that directly address the issues associated with being an incarcerated mother are essential. The chance to earn overnight visiting privileges with their children can be a powerful incentive for women to participate in parenting classes.

In addition to these more structured programs, other less formal activities, such as writing letters, making phone calls, and attending craft classes for gift-making, enable mothers to maintain contact with their children.

Parole Plan

In the final phase of incarceration, an inmate develops a comprehensive parole plan in conjunction with her case manager. The parole plan should address her continuing education, work, family, social, and recreational goals to be achieved while in work release or on parole.

Work Release

Continued support during the work release phase of incarceration is essential to an inmate's successful transition to the community. Links to continuing education and job development assistance are critical to ensure she will have the opportunity to practice the skills she worked hard to achieve while incarcerated.

Employability and a decent working wage are critical to a newly released inmate's ability to re-establish family and community ties. Substance abuse, mental health, and other counseling services are also likely to be required if the inmate is to meet the goals of her parole plan.

Building New Facilities

Building a new women's facility offers a unique opportunity. Ideally, the facility should emphasize privacy, dignity, and self-sufficiency. These goals are enhanced when the design provides for small living units with personal services located close to or in the living unit itself.

Additionally, a housing assignment system that places inmates with similar profiles together reduces the potential for friction, thus contributing to a more peaceful, safe living environment. A housing unit subdivided into a number of "pods," with integral program and support spaces allows women to live in small, manageable groups that foster a sense of community and accountability.

A calm atmosphere (with architectural features such as generous use of glazing to permit natural light, use of color and texture, and comfortable, durable furnishings), in conjunction with the administration's clearly stated behavioral expectations, enhances the manageability and personal growth of the occupants.

Women serving long prison terms prefer the privacy of their own cells or rooms. Small lounges in addition to dayrooms allow women to choose between interaction with a small or large group. Kitchenettes and beverage areas with refrigerators promote positive socialization skills and give women the opportunity to practice independent living skills. Laundry and personal grooming areas located nearby support inmates' personal dignity.

Program space can be designed to incorporate special programs. Vocational training and industries spaces can be designed for flexibility to accommodate changing demands for skills in the job market.

Operating a women's facility designed specifically for the population offers a tremendous opportunity for making the environment treatment-oriented. Less emphasis on expensive architectural and security features, inappropriate for most female inmates' custody levels, enables correctional administrators to focus on innovative management and programming.

In the long run, a wide array of programs and services designed to meet the unique characteristics of the female offender population benefits both the correctional system and the community by releasing women who can contribute positively to their families and communities.

References

Bureau of Justice Statistics. 1988. *Sourcebook of Criminal Justice Statistics, 1987.* Washington, D.C.: U.S. Government Printing Office.

Feihman, Claire. 1983. An historical overview of the treatment of incarcerated women: Myths and realities of rehabilitation. *Prison Journal* V(63):12-26.

VIII.

HIV, AIDS, and the Female Offender

by W. Travis Lawson, Jr., M.D., and Lt. Lena Sue Fawkes

In 1990, the number of reported acquired immunodeficiency syndrome (AIDS) cases among women in the United States exceeded 15,000, an increase of 34 percent from 1989 and approximately 9 percent of all adult AIDS cases in the United States. As the AIDS epidemic approaches its second decade, both the number of new infections with HIV (the human immunodeficiency virus that causes the disease) and the number of full-blown AIDS cases or cases of AIDS-related complex (ARC) are expected to continue to rise sharply for the next few years in the United States and worldwide. At least one drug, AZT, may slow the progression of the HIV infection. In addition, there are medications to treat certain opportunistic diseases to which people with AIDS are susceptible.

Nevertheless, the Centers for Disease Control (CDC) estimates that one million Americans are infected with HIV, most of them with no symptoms and no knowledge that they are carriers. Another seven to ten million people around the world are also infected, according to estimates by the World Health Organization. At the end of 1990, more than 150,000 Americans had been diagnosed with AIDS, two-thirds of whom have since died. The CDC estimates that by the end of 1993, 390,000 to 480,000 Americans will have been diagnosed with AIDS—with between 285,000 and 340,000 deaths.

AIDS is no longer primarily the affliction of well-defined risk groups. In particular, heterosexual transmission is on the rise—though it still accounts for a relatively small percentage of U.S. cases, it is the predominant mode of spread in most countries. Among American heterosexuals, sexual partners of intravenous drug users and people who have multiple partners remain at greatest risk.

Epidemiology of HIV Infection in Women

According to data published by the CDC, as of January 1989, 52 percent of women diagnosed with AIDS in the United States are intravenous drug users, 30

W. Travis Lawson, Jr., M.D., is associate warden of clinical programs at the Federal Medical Center in Lexington, Kentucky.

Lt. Lena Sue Fawkes, USPHS, CRNA, MSN, is quality assurance coordinator at the Federal Medical Center, Lexington, Kentucky.

percent were exposed to HIV through heterosexual contact, and 11 percent received HIV-infected blood or blood products. The transmission category for the remaining 7 percent is "undetermined." A significant trend noted between 1982 and 1986, however, is the one-hundred-fold increase in the percentage of female cases of AIDS classified as heterosexually transmitted. The number of females infected by the virus increased 100 percent again between 1986 and 1992.

About half of the women with AIDS in the United States are aged 30 to 39; 90 percent of adult female cases occur in women aged 20 to 50. CDC data underscore HIV's disproportionate impact on minority populations. Although 17 percent of all women in the United States are black or Hispanic, blacks and Hispanics account for 73 percent (52 percent and 21 percent, respectively) of reported AIDS cases among women. This number reflects the prevalence of intravenous drug use in some black and Hispanic communities, particularly on the East Coast. Although most states have reported adult female AIDS cases to the CDC, more than half of these cases have been reported from the northeastern states, and half of all cases reported in the East Coast were in New York alone.

Fifty-nine percent of women with AIDS reported to the CDC have subsequently died, compared with 50 percent of men. AIDS has a significant impact on mortality patterns for women in areas where HIV infection is common; it has now become the leading cause of death for women aged 30 to 34 in New York City.

The virus that causes AIDS may be more common among prison and jail inmates, especially women, than previously thought, according to a study based on testing of nearly 11,000 inmates entering ten prisons and jails between mid-1988 and mid-1989. The study, conducted by the Johns Hopkins School of Public Health and the CDC found that rates of HIV infection ranged from 2.1 to 7.6 percent for male inmates and from 2.5 to 14.7 percent among female inmates. At nine of the ten correctional facilities, women had higher rates of HIV infection than men. The difference was greatest among inmates under age 25, with 5.2 percent of women in that age group testing positive, compared with 2.3 percent of the men. Minority groups also had higher rates of infection: 4.8 percent overall, compared with 2.5 percent of white inmates. No major difference in HIV infection rates was found between prisons and jails.

A vast majority of adults with HIV infection are in their reproductive years. According to CDC data, the risk factor for about 78 percent of the children who have AIDS in the United States is a parent with AIDS or in an AIDS risk group.

It is assumed that these children were born to infected mothers and were infected themselves during the perinatal period. The relative risk of HIV infection to the fetus of an infected woman is not known. In an early study of infected mothers who had previously delivered infants who developed AIDS, 57 percent (six of fourteen) of babies born subsequently were also infected. In contrast, no babies born to women impregnated by artificial insemination showed evidence of HIV infection after one year of followup. (Because these were small studies, it is important to emphasize that the risk estimates are varied and uncertain.)

At this time, outcomes for the newborn cannot be predicted by the clinical status of the mother during pregnancy. Infected babies have been born to women who are HIV-positive but have not developed symptoms, as well as to mothers with AIDS and ARC. A mother with AIDS can also deliver a baby with no evidence of disease. Transmission from an infected woman to older children or to other household members who are not her sexual partners has never been documented.

HIV Infection and AIDS in Correctional Facilities

While the crisis atmosphere surrounding AIDS in prisons and jails seems to have dissipated, the disease remains a serious issue for correctional administrators. Concern has shifted significantly from short-term matters, such as fear of casual transmission, to "long-haul" issues, such as housing, programming, and medical care for inmates who have HIV infection.

As the population ages, and as determinate sentencing and strict sentencing guidelines continue, inmates—in particular, women—will age within our facilities. We will see more and more women of childbearing age who are infected. The historic differences between the federal offender versus offenders within state, city, or county systems have become blurred by the issue of drug trafficking. These offenders tend to be less educated and from predominantly urban and depressed socioeconomic backgrounds. The frequent victimization of these female offenders also increases the risk for heterosexual disease transmission.

During its first appearance within the correctional setting, AIDS victims were predominantly white homosexual or bisexual males; however, heterosexuals and minorities are now being infected in increasing numbers. In society, the disease currently has a greater impact on the intravenous (IV) drug user population than on the homosexual community. In the Bureau of Prisons, a considerable percentage of present and future inmates will come from backgrounds of IV drug use or will have had intimate contact with IV drug users. Although current data suggest a 1 percent seropositive rate of HIV infection (a composite infection rate, slightly less for males and slightly more for females, using current Bureau of Prisons monitoring standards), this still exceeds the estimated seroprevalence within the at-large population of 0.005 percent.

Evaluating Female Offenders

IV drug users in treatment programs and those who have the physical signs of IV drug use are at risk for HIV infection. Other women at risk, however, are not so easily identified. A comprehensive patient history will help identify some women at risk. Appropriate questions can be inserted into the social, sexual, and medical portions of the history. These sensitive matters may then be documented in a way that maximizes confidentiality. These follow-up questions are suggested to help determine the prevalence of the virus in female inmate patients:

1. Have you ever been tested for antibodies to the AIDS virus? If so, what was the result of your test? When and why were you tested?
2. Since the late 1970s, have you ever injected drugs into your body with a needle? If yes, have you shared needles with other people?" (If a woman is or has been an IV drug user, a history of the type of drugs

used and the extent of drug use and needle sharing should be obtained.)

3. Since 1979, have you ever had sexual relations with a person at risk for AIDS—someone who injects drugs, a gay or bisexual man, a hemophiliac, or a person from Haiti or Central Africa? (If yes, further history should be taken on the clinical status of the person at risk, the type of sexual activity involved, the duration of the relationship, and the use and type of contraception.)

4. Have you had any anonymous sexual partners or partners that you did not know well who may possibly have been in AIDS risk groups? (Many women do not know the risk status of all their sexual partners. The question is most relevant if the patient lives where HIV infection is common.)

5. Have you tried to become pregnant through artificial insemination since the late 1970s? If yes, where? (Again, this question is most relevant if the patient lives where HIV infection is common.)

6. Have you received a transfusion of blood or blood products since 1979? (If yes, ask when, where, and how much blood. The risk is higher if a woman received a transfusion before 1985 in an area where HIV was common.)

7. Are you from Haiti or Central Africa?

8. Is there any other reason why you think you might be at risk of exposure to HIV? (This question may lead to the patient revealing an additional possible risk factor, such as providing health care to people with AIDS or HIV infection. The question also gives the woman a chance to express her fears about AIDS so that the health care worker can evaluate her needs for information.)

Even when such histories are taken, not all women at risk will be identified. Many women are unaware of the drug use or unsafe sexual activities of their current or past sexual partners.

Clinical Issues

The signs and symptoms of HIV infection are the same for women as for men, with one notable exception: Women rarely develop Kaposi's sarcoma (KS), the most common AIDS-related malignancy. Women with AIDS most frequently develop pneumocystis carinii pneumonia (PCP), the most common AIDS-related opportunistic infection.

Few studies have been published on aspects of HIV infection that may be unique to women. However, some studies have revealed a high percentage of women with gynecological disorders as well as very high maternal morbidity and mortality rates. Whether these findings were related to HIV infection or to other patient characteristics (such as IV drug abuse and poverty) has not been adequately addressed. Another study reported that women with clinical manifestations of HIV infection had a greater tendency to be inaccurately diagnosed, despite numerous medical evaluations. Given the preponderance of infected men, routes of HIV infection in women had not been proven to be statistically relevant until recently.

Pregnancy, which is associated with changes in cellular immunity, may affect both the natural history of HIV infection and the development of AIDS-related disease. One study followed fifteen women who had no symptoms of AIDS or HIV at childbirth for thirty months after their deliveries. During the follow-up period, five of these women developed AIDS, seven developed related symptoms, and only three remained asymptomatic. Still, while there remains a theoretical risk that pregnancy could accelerate progression of HIV disease, controlled studies following both pregnant and non-pregnant seropositive women are needed to answer the question.

A number of case reports discuss women who develop AIDS-related opportunistic infections while pregnant. These women's diseases progressed rapidly; they died within weeks of diagnosis. Some symptoms of HIV infection are similar to those commonly seen in problem pregnancies—fatigue, anorexia, weight loss, and shortness of breath. Health care workers caring for pregnant women in HIV risk groups must assess these women carefully for signs of HIV infection.

Counseling Women with HIV Infection

Counseling issues differ for women depending on whether they are uninfected but at risk for HIV infection, seropositive but asymptomatic, or have full-blown HIV infection or AIDS.

Women at risk should be counseled on how HIV is transmitted and on how to avoid or minimize their exposures. Programs designed to meet the needs of women at risk who are or may become pregnant should make the HIV antibody test understandable and readily available. The CDC recommends antibody testing for women at high risk but emphasizes that many women are unaware of their risks. The most important part of any such program is identifying women at risk and educating them to prevent exposure to (and transmission of) HIV infection. The best way to prevent transmission of HIV to infants is to prevent its transmission to women.

The concerns expressed most frequently by seropositive women are fear of becoming ill, fear of transmitting HIV to their sexual partners and children, difficulty in communicating with potential sexual partners and in remaining sexually active, and not being able to bear children for fear they will become infected.

The CDC recommends that seropositive women avoid pregnancy until more is known about HIV transmission during pregnancy. This recommendation is often difficult to accept. Even more difficult is the situation of a woman who is already pregnant and then learns that she is infected with HIV. Although transmission to the infant is neither inevitable nor predictable, its likelihood is high. Infected pregnant women who do not elect to have an abortion will need extensive counseling and support.

The issues that women who have symptomatic HIV infection and AIDS must deal with overlap those of asymptomatic seropositives and women at risk. Fear of transmitting HIV to others is a major concern. Unlike women in the other groups, those who have symptomatic HIV infection and AIDS must deal with grief over the loss of their previous body image, sexual freedom, and potential for childbearing. They must also come to grips with the imminent loss of their own lives. Grief and other emotions triggered by an ARC or AIDS diagnosis can be profound.

Women who have symptomatic HIV infection and AIDS experience a unique social isolation. Although women were among the first persons diagnosed with AIDS, they are still not widely perceived as at risk for AIDS, which is seen as a "man's disease." Moreover, women with AIDS are a diverse group with no parallel community to look to for support, as homosexual men can. Very few programs have services designed for women with AIDS.

For some women, being diagnosed with symptomatic HIV disease or AIDS is the first indication that their sexual partners are infected and that these partners are therefore probably IV drug users or bisexuals. The anger and sense of betrayal add to the emotional crisis provoked by the diagnosis.

Because most women suffering from AIDS are in their childbearing years, many already have children. A major concern of such women is care for their children if they become disabled or die. Many infected women are also poor and have had to deal with the problems associated with poverty—inadequate housing, poor nutrition, lack of health care and child care—long before their diagnosis. All of these problems are exacerbated by the diagnosis.

Women who have symptomatic HIV disease and AIDS are often part of households already dealing with the disease: their children and sexual partners may be infected. When AIDS affects an entire family, the psychosocial needs are extensive.

Conclusion

AIDS is a complex, challenging, and tragic issue. It is even more challenging for incarcerated women. The HIV epidemic will continue to influence the custodial and medical missions in correctional facilities in the future. This mandates that the correctional system must stay abreast of developments in this area. National population projections over the next ten years notwithstanding, correctional populations will continue to rise. The demographics of those at risk tell us that AIDS will be a significant part of correctional medicine through the coming decade.

IX.

Pregnant Offenders: Profile and Special Problems

by T. A. Ryan, Ph.D., and James B. Grassano, M.C.J.

The pregnant female adult offender has become a topic of increasing interest and concern in the past decade. Historically, female offenders have received much less attention than male offenders. However, the rate of population growth for female adult inmates has exceeded that of male adult inmates each year since 1981. From 1980 to 1989 the male population increased by 112 percent and the female population by 202 percent (Bureau of Justice Statistics 1991). In spite of these statistics, relatively little empirical research on female offenders has been conducted.

Literature on Female Offenders

Considering that empirical research on female offenders in general is limited, it is not surprising to find an almost total absence of information on incarcerated adult pregnant offenders. Literature on the female offender contains a small amount of information related to pregnant incarcerated offenders and almost no information concerning mother-child relations. Prior to Ryan and Grassano's 1988 study on pregnant adult offenders, only one comprehensive study had been reported, and it focused primarily on the health care of incarcerated pregnant offenders.

Ward and Kassebaum (1965) reported that compared with the sociological literature on men's prisons, little was known about the social organization of women's prisons. Klein (1973) noted that the study of female criminality had been neglected. Noblit (1976) observed there was a lack of research and theory on women and crime. With the exception of the classic study of 500 delinquent women (Glueck & Glueck 1934), there were little scientifically collected and analyzed data on adult female offenders prior to the 1980s. Holt (1982) observed female offenders had been constantly overlooked in litigation by or on behalf of adult inmates in general. Holt took the position that size of inmate population was a determining factor in allocation of funds. Small female offender populations

T. A. Ryan, Ph.D., is president of Ryan Associates, Inc., in Lexington, South Carolina.

James B. Grassano, M.C.J., is research associate of Ryan Associates, Inc., in Lexington, South Carolina.

resulted in inadequate funding, administrative stumbling blocks, and neglect of female offenders' needs.

However, there have been studies done on female offenders and their relationship with their children. A study by Boudouris (1985) examined the history of programs for children of inmates. Boudouris listed seven programs used within fifty-seven institutions throughout the United States. Although not every program was used in each institution, Boudouris found that 96.5 percent of the fifty-seven institutions included in the study conducted classes for inmates with children. Eighty-one percent of these institutions gave furloughs to mothers with children, 40 percent had children's centers within the institutions, 37 percent allowed conjugal visits, 9 percent developed community facilities for mothers and children, and 2 percent had prison nurseries.

Literature on Pregnant Female Offenders

Holt (1982) examined legal aspects of pregnant offenders. A few court cases have addressed the care and treatment of the addicted pregnant offender. Although no precedents resulted from these cases (as all have been settled by consent decree), the focus of this litigation has been to improve medical services for these high-risk pregnant women.

Some studies have been conducted on the type and availability of programs for pregnant offenders. Ayers and Johnson (1987) collected data from forty-two facilities for female offenders. The study sought information about the types of services available to pregnant inmates. The study also focused on the types of professionals, facilities, and programs that are used in providing these needs.

The findings from Ayers and Johnson revealed that health care services were present in 92 percent of the forty-two prisons surveyed. Prenatal care in 87 percent of the prisons began within two weeks after the symptoms of pregnancy were reported. Of the responding institutions, 50 percent offered prenatal care classes within the institution. However, most of the prenatal care classes were voluntary. All of the responding institutions reported that they did not provide for birth within the institution. As for training for natural childbirth, the majority of inmates could participate in natural childbirth if they desired.

Profile of Pregnant Adult Offenders

The national concern for addressing drug-related problems has focused attention on addicted pregnant inmates. The effect of drug addiction during pregnancy on newborns has greatly increased interest in pregnant adult offenders. As many as 375,000 newborns a year may be affected by substance abuse in the United States, according to Dr. Ira Charnoff, president of the National Association for Perinatal Addiction Research and Education (American Bar Association 1989). This statistic reveals an increased interest in and concern about pregnant offenders, particularly the effect of substance abuse on both mother and fetus, reflected by litigation, statutes, standards, and guidelines.

Ryan (1988) examined adult female offenders in state correctional institutions. The population studied consisted of adult offenders in correctional institutions only and did not include those in detention, prerelease, and pretrial. Data were collected on 18,651 female offenders. The sample was drawn from the American Correctional Association's, *Directory of Juvenile and Adult Correctional Departments, Institutions, Agencies, and Paroling Authorities*, which listed 103 facilities with adult female offenders; 71 of these facilities provided information for the study.

The demographic profile of pregnant offenders does not differ significantly from the national profile of female offenders. The survey revealed that 2 percent of the adult female offenders studied were pregnant. Of this 2 percent, 22 percent were institutionalized in minimum security, 22 percent were in minimum security with work release/pass/furlough, 26 percent were in medium security, 19 percent were in maximum security, and 11 percent were housed in close security.

The survey also revealed that 82 percent of pregnant offenders were between 18 and 30 years of age. Forty-two percent of pregnant offenders were black, and 47 percent were white (11 percent were from other ethnic backgrounds, including Hispanic, Native American, and Asian). The survey indicated that 58 percent were single, 7 percent were divorced, 11 percent were separated, 1 percent were widowed, and 23 percent were married.

Fifteen percent were convicted for an offense toward persons, 45 percent committed a property offense, 21 percent had a substance abuse violation, 12 percent were convicted for drug sales, 4 percent committed vice/morals crimes, and 3 percent committed other crimes not listed here. Half of the female offenders surveyed already had at least two children. Twenty-five percent of the women had three or more children. Twenty-four percent had not previously borne children. One percent had an unknown number of previously borne children.

The results indicated that no babies were delivered in a correctional facility: 99 percent of the babies were delivered in a community hospital and 1 percent of the babies were delivered in a university hospital. The survey results also indicated that 43 percent of the babies born to pregnant offenders were taken at birth, 53 percent remained with the mother for up to one week, 1 percent remained with the mother one week to one month, 1 percent remained with the mother six months to one year.

Problems of Pregnant Adult Offenders

Female offenders have special problems arising from or associated with pregnancy or pregnancy-related conditions. These problems have resulted in lawsuits and attempts to establish standards, guidelines, or regulations governing pregnant offenders. Pregnancy-related problems are not limited to concerns that arise during the offender's admission to the facility. Rather, there are problems at all stages of pregnancy during incarceration. Mills and Barrett (1990) noted that concerns for high-risk pregnant offenders included use of shackles and restraints, transportation methods, and drug addiction. These women are presenting the greatest health service challenge that jails have ever encountered.

Women who are not incarcerated tend to be worried and concerned about the complications involved with pregnancy and childbirth. Pregnant women on trial may worry about pregnancy to the point of confession to a crime they did not commit to secure medical care for themselves and their fetus. The concerns about pregnancy may result in a woman on trial entering a plea motivated by her pregnancy that is not entirely voluntary (Holt 1982).

Pregnant inmates may suffer mental or emotional problems. Often the baby is illegitimate and unwanted. The right to choose between carrying the fetus to term or terminating the pregnancy may be denied to pregnant inmates. Prison officials have been reported to have used coercion to force inmates to abort the unborn fetus. On the other hand, inmates desiring abortion may be denied the request (Holt 1982).

Pregnant inmates may encounter many injustices in the prison system during their incarceration. They may not be offered a special diet, including high protein, iron, milk, and vitamins. They may be confined to cells and thus denied the necessary exercise required during pregnancy. Work assignments may not be appropriate for pregnant women. Holt (1982) reported one case of a woman with a history of miscarriages forced to perform rigorous janitorial work. She requested lighter work assignments, but the request was denied. She gave birth to a stillborn infant.

Also, a routine part of admissions in most correctional facilities is the strip search. Holt (1982) noted that this may involve a full internal pelvic examination. For a pregnant woman, if such a search is conducted without medical justification, it may increase the possibility of vaginal and cervical irritation and infection.

In some instances, a physical examination is not given to female offenders on admission to a facility, thus precluding early abortion and/or prenatal care. Holt (1982) notes that medical care may not be available at the correctional facility. One survey of twenty-six institutions for women reported only eight had medical care on the premises twenty-four hours a day (Resnik & Shaw 1980). Ryan (1984) found seventeen out of forty-five institutions had twenty-four-hour medical service on premises.

Other issues facing pregnant offenders include whether prison nurseries should be established, if the children of these inmates should be allowed to live in the institution to remain close to their mothers, and if day care centers should be provided while mothers visit with other adults.

Drug addiction poses major problems for pregnant offenders. Institutions have been concerned about mothers giving birth while addicted to drugs and the liability of the institution in these cases. The fetus' brain also develops tolerance and dependence to drugs in the same manner as the maternal brain. Special detoxification programs should be implemented. Pregnant addicts have been forced to go through withdrawal without consideration of the fetus, though withdrawal symptoms are also experienced by the fetus (Holt 1982). Since fetal withdrawal in-utero carries a high risk of morbidity and morality, it is important to prevent its occurrence through careful, slow detoxification or maintenance therapy. The problem of addicted pregnant offenders is complex and merits special attention.

There may be problems associated with delivery for the pregnant offender. Pregnant offenders may not be provided with adequate information about options for childbirth methods. Holt (1982) reports surgery being performed resulting in infertility more often than necessary. Many institutions lack delivery facilities.

When transfer is made to a community hospital, this may not be done in a timely manner. The problem of postpartum recuperation for offenders frequently is hampered by immediate removal of the newborn from the mother.

Conclusion

The profile of incarcerated pregnant offenders in the United States clearly establishes the fact that this group represents a special needs population of female offenders. The problems unique to the condition of pregnancy within a correctional institution are complex and critical, deserving of attention and resources that in the past have for the most part not been forthcoming.

References

American Bar Association. 1989. Crime and pregnancy. *American Bar Association Journal* 75:14-16.

American Correctional Association. 1988. *Directory of juvenile and adult correctional departments, institutions, and paroling authorities.* College Park, Md: American Correctional Association.

Ayers, K., and F. Johnson. 1987. *Health care of pregnant inmates.* Owensboro, Ky.: Kentucky Wesleyan College Criminal Justice Research Center.

Boudouris, J. 1985. *Prisons and kids.* College Park, Md.: American Correctional Association.

Bureau of Justice Statistics. 1991. *Women in prison.* Washington, D.C.: Bureau of Justice Statistics.

Glueck, S., and E. Glueck. 1934. *Five hundred delinquent women.* New York: Alfred A. Knopf.

Holt, K. E. 1982. Nine months to live—The law and the pregnant inmate. *Journal of Family Law* 20 (3): 523-42.

Klein, D. 1973. The etiology of female crime. *Issues in Criminology* 8 (2): 3-30.

Mills, R., and H. Barrett. 1990. Meeting the special challenge of providing health care to women inmates in the '90s. *American Jails* 4 (September-October) 55-57.

Noblit, G. W. 1976. Women and crime, 1960-1970. *Social Science Quarterly* 56: 650-57.

Resnik, J., and N. Shaw. 1980. Prisoners' of their sex: Health problems of incarcerated women. In *Prisoner's rights sourcebook II*, ed. I. P. Robbins, 372-83. New York: Clark Boardman.

Ryan, T. A. 1984. *Adult female offenders and institutional programs: A state of the art analysis.* Washington, D.C.: U. S. Department of Justice.

Ryan, T. A. 1988. *Profile of adult female offenders and programs and services provided for these offenders.* Columbia, S. C.: University of South Carolina.

Ryan, T. A., and J. B. Grassano. 1988. *Survey of pregnant adult offenders.* Columbia, S.C.: University of South Carolina.

Ward, D. A., and C. G. Kassebaum. 1965. *Women's prison: Sex and social structure.* Chicago: Aldine Publishers.

X.

Care of the Pregnant Offender

by Anita G. Hufft, Ph.D., Lt. Lena Sue Fawkes,
and W. Travis Lawson, Jr., M.D.

Women face many choices when they are pregnant. Even deciding to find out whether they are pregnant can be an overwhelming experience for some women. Whether to continue the pregnancy, how to manage it, and how to select a particular childbirth method largely depends on the knowledge, attitudes, and disposition of people close to the pregnant woman.

While medical literature provides detailed guidelines on monitoring the fetus and performing appropriate medical procedures during labor and birth, there are few guidelines for addressing the psychological issues associated with childbirth.

Pregnant women in prison face unique problems. Stress, environmental and legal restrictions, unhealthy behavior, and weakened or nonexistent social support systems—all common among female inmates—have an even greater effect on pregnant inmates.

Maternity care in the prison setting is based on the following values and assumptions:

1. Pregnancy is a healthy state in which biological, psychological, emotional, and intellectual adaptations to one's surroundings increase the likelihood of giving birth to a healthy baby.
2. Every pregnant woman has the right of self-determination regarding her body and its functions.
3. Every woman has the right to physical safety and access to certain health care services. Ensuring the safety of the pregnant woman may warrant expanding her movement privileges and access to certain health care services. Staff access to previous health care records may be restricted. Violent or self-destructive women must be evaluated to ensure they are competent to select health care choices.

Anita G. Hufft, Ph.D., RN, is an associate professor and campus dean of the Indiana University School of Nursing in New Albany, Indiana and a consultant to the Federal Medical Center, Lexington, Kentucky.

Lt. Lena Sue Fawkes, USPHS, CRNA, MSN, is quality assurance coordinator at Federal Medical Center, Lexington.

W. Travis Lawson, Jr., M.D., is associate warden of clinical programs at Federal Medical Center, Lexington.

Prison and the Experience of Mothering

All of the "tasks" of pregnancy are affected by incarceration. Women in prison are placed outside the normal mothering experience in four ways:

1. Stress—Incarcerated women experience higher than normal levels of stress. They have a higher incidence of complications during pregnancy, labor, and delivery. Many have not practiced good health habits throughout their lives. Infants of incarcerated women are more likely to have life-threatening problems at birth, contract serious illnesses, and be exposed to a negative social environment as they grow into childhood.
2. Restricted environment—Adaptation to pregnancy is limited by the prison environment. Mandatory work, structured meal times, and lack of environmental stimulation may decrease the likelihood of individualized prenatal care. For instance, pregnant inmates receive standard clothing that often does not fit well. Alternatives for special clothing (e.g., stockings and shoes) may be dictated by availability in the institution or by what family and friends are willing to supply. In addition, disciplinary action or other restrictions may interfere with the offender's adaptation to pregnancy.
3. Altered social support systems—Even if ideal opportunities for nutritional education and physical development are available during pregnancy, pregnant women will not take advantage of them if they do not receive support from their inmate peer groups. Limited health care facilities sometimes warrant the immediate transfer of a pregnant inmate to a civilian hospital at the onset of labor. But that inmate will then miss the presence of a support person. These limitations may place certain mothers at risk for longer labor, induce those in labor not to seek care soon enough, or increase the discomfort of labor and the need for medical intervention.
4. Altered maternal roles—Maternal identity depends on rehearsal for the anticipated role after birth. Women in federal and most state prisons do not directly care for their infants after birth. Developing a maternal role therefore depends on the mother's plans for the infant after birth. The inmate can place the infant either for adoption or for guardianship. She may choose to maintain a maternal role in absentia or relinquish that role to a relative or friend, depending on factors such as support systems in prison, the inmate's self-esteem and problem-solving skills, the presence of an intact family on the outside, and the imminence of release.

Women who expect to give up their infants after birth do not experience bonding in the same way as mothers who know they will keep their babies. In addition to losing freedom, privacy, and self-esteem while incarcerated, inmates must also cope with losing a child and an identity as a mother. The ability to sacrifice one's own needs for another's is tested during the mothering experience. Whether the nurturing role is innate or learned, most women relate childbirth with infant care. Removing this nurturing role from the woman in prison may trigger feelings of dependence, a loss of self-esteem, an inability to focus on the future, or self-destructive behavior.

Plans for the female inmate's maternity and nursing care should therefore be guided by plans to reduce stress, to decrease environmental restrictions, to promote a healthy lifestyle, and to develop decision-making and coping skills for resolving infant placement problems and assuming a maternal role after the birth.

Preparation for birth and care of the infant includes teaching the mother decision-making skills. Counseling should emphasize developing an identity during pregnancy and strategies for coping with the loss of the infant. After the birth, the mother will need counseling to make and accept the decision to place the infant for adoption or temporary guardianship.

For the medical staff, helping the pregnant inmate to resolve the placement of an infant after birth is based on accurately assessing the infant's potential family environment and the psychological state of the mother.

If the inmate is successful in coping with pregnancy and childbirth, she may have learned the skills necessary to successfully cope with her remaining period of imprisonment. Comprehensive maternity care for the pregnant inmate is one component of a supportive prison environment for the female offender.

The Clinical Dilemma

Recognizing that a small percentage of pregnancies have poor outcomes, doctors introduced the concept of "high-risk pregnancy" into clinical medicine. Identifying high-risk pregnancies allows doctors to intensively monitor all stages of the pregnancy. How do doctors recognize high-risk pregnancies?

Within the setting of the Federal Bureau of Prisons and similar correctional systems, a majority of pregnant inmates meet some of the criteria for being high-risk. Correctional systems have traditionally defined the high-risk female inmate as one who is a minority, is older than 35 years, and has a history of chemical dependency, multiple abortions or miscarriages, and/or sexually transmitted diseases or pelvic inflammatory disease, among other factors. A single major medical condition, or several minor conditions, can predict a less-than-favorable birth. Such pregnancies must be termed high-risk, and these patients should be cared for in specially designed and staffed centers.

The presence of high-risk pregnancies in the federal system increases the importance of prioritizing the needs of pregnant inmates—allowing individuals at lesser risk to be treated at the institution or in the community and those at significant risk to be treated at a referral facility for more intensive care. The Federal Medical Center in Lexington, Kentucky, is uniquely capable of offering medical care for high-risk inmates. Lexington has an accredited hospital closely affiliated with the physicians and services of the University of Kentucky Medical Center. In addition, Lexington can house inmates of all security levels.

Monitoring of high-risk pregnant inmates should not be ignored by facilities that do not view as part of their role the care of pregnant offenders. All facilities can prudently meet the challenges of monitoring these inmates with proper planning and resources. Appropriate budgetary resources to care for the pregnant offender can be allocated during the facility's strategic planning process.

The Social Network during Pregnancy

Misguided advice about pregnancy impedes access to and use of prenatal care for low-income women. Low-income women who are less educated and often exploited are less likely to comply with reliable prenatal health care advice. The prison population is an "invented family" for the pregnant inmate. Membership in this subgroup is often attained through an inmate "mentor," who offers advice and makes recommendations regarding acceptable practices during pregnancy.

Convenience is often cited as a reason pregnant women rely on peers rather than professional health care personnel for advice. The prison subculture is a unique mix of racial, religious, and social customs and practices aimed at organizing the activities of inmates, both within and outside the system. An inmate's reference group includes family, friends, and acquaintances, who serve as a resource for acceptable information, including medical advice. This group plays a major role in the pregnant inmate's interpretation of symptoms, self-diagnosis, the need for clinical appointments, use of self-remedies, evaluation of treatment, and belief in professional explanations.

The health and lifestyle choices of pregnant inmates are determined by prison subcultures as well as inherited cultural practices. The healthcare practitioner's thorough assessment of factors affecting pregnancy should include identifying groups and persons to whom the patient turns for information. While such networks can detract from the quality of health care, they can also reinforce medical advice. Knowing where the pregnant inmate information sources lie will help the health care practitioner use prison resources in the broadest sense possible. Pregnant inmates frequently turn to their networks for advice on the following topics:

- diet and nutrition
- activity and hygiene
- harmful substances or practices to avoid
- remedies for the discomforts of pregnancy
- when to seek advice about professional medical care
- information on labor and delivery

This list suggests a pattern for dialogue with the patient. Initial and follow-up visits should include this information, in this order, to get the patient's attention and to allow the practitioner to explore factors that may influence her compliance with medical advice. The physician should frankly and clearly explain the consequences of noncompliance in a nonthreatening manner, emphasizing physician-patient cooperation for a successful pregnancy. Physicians should also ask about important medical issues such as substance abuse and high-risk sexual practices in their initial assessments of the pregnant client.

Studies suggest that health education should be vigorously extended not only to the pregnant inmate, but to her reference groups. Peers should be viewed as allies, not liabilities, in the reinforcement of good medical advice. Routine counseling and education by health care providers to all inmates dispels misinformation and the stress it causes for pregnant inmates.

Satisfaction with Maternity Care

A patient's satisfaction with her medical care is often cited as the indicator of the quality of that care. By examining the inmate's satisfaction with her maternity care, quality assurance indicators can be developed. Pregnant women, in general, are often afraid to voice their dissatisfaction with their maternity care in fear that their opinion will adversely affect further care. The female inmate is even more fearful: she is in a controlled environment in which every action may affect her well-being. Even though pregnant inmates may complain about prenatal care, they are equally negative in their description of pregnancy and birth experiences. Part of this negative attitude may be due to a transference of feelings regarding their care to feelings regarding their birth experience.

For quality control, it may be better to measure the availability of satisfying conditions and the frequency of doctor-patient contact rather than to measure patient responses directly.

Patient dissatisfaction results from displeasure or disagreement with the maternity care the patient actually experiences compared with the care she had expected. The stress the pregnant inmate experiences as a result of unmet expectations increases her risk of health problems during pregnancy, labor, and birth. Therefore, ensuring the quality of maternity services in prisons should include measures to increase patient satisfaction.

Conditions for positive pregnancies and childbirths include the following:

1. The inmate should be allowed to participate in decisionmaking.
2. Thorough explanations should be given to the mother (especially for delivery by caesarean section) on what she can expect during her pregnancy and childbirth. This provides the pregnant inmate with emotional support from the physician and nurses.
3. The nurse and doctor should be responsive to the woman's pain.
4. Inmates should have only a short time spent waiting on appointments.

The halo effect—"satisfaction with care must make satisfaction with delivery"—does not hold up. Most studies collecting data within two months after delivery tend to rate the delivery experience and maternity care very highly. Satisfaction with care decreases, however, when women are interviewed more than two months after delivery.

Team Delivery of Services

A holistic, health-oriented model is the framework that guides the delivery of health services to pregnant inmates in federal correctional facilities. The coordinator for maternity health services supervises the activities of staff physicians, consulting physicians, physician assistants, social workers, and nurses. Referral to specialized services is performed as required by the patient's needs and institutional policy.

The formulation of an obstetrical treatment plan for pregnant inmates is the responsibility of several different health care workers. The way such individuals work as a team affects the success of the treatment plan and ultimately the health of the mother and infant.

The attending physician or chief obstetrical physician serves as team leader. He or she can make medical diagnoses that prioritize treatment needs. Other health care needs can be met (as deemed appropriate by the team leader) through interdisciplinary contributions to the treatment plan. While this model is common, it is not always the most reliable, for it depends on the availability of staff and the patient's needs. The use of other health care professionals to manage treatment planning and intervention may represent a better use of resources.

The patient herself is also an integral part of the treatment team's setting of health care goals and determination of treatment plans. When a patient is allowed to work with the medical team in setting goals, compliance with treatment is likely to be greater.

XI.

Incarcerated Mothers and Their Children: Maintaining Family Ties

by Barbara Bloom

Parents who are in prison face many problems in maintaining meaningful relationships with their children. This is especially true for incarcerated mothers. Indeed, families are more likely to be disrupted by women's incarceration than by men's (Baugh 1985; Datesman & Cales 1983).

The Bureau of Justice Statistics (BJS) reported that 76 percent of incarcerated women in America were mothers in 1986. Nine out of ten of these mothers had children under the age of eighteen, and six out of ten had more than one child (BJS 1991).

By its very nature, imprisonment has an adverse effect on mother-infant bonding. In most instances, mothers are allowed to spend only a few days with their babies after delivery. Essential bonding cannot occur in such a short period of time, and this has serious deleterious implications on the future mother-child relationship (McGowan & Blumenthal 1978; Bloom 1989).

The children of incarcerated mothers also experience special problems. In most cases where mothers are living with children prior to incarceration, the separation caused by imprisonment is a major trauma for the children. Separation between mothers and their young children may lead to emotional, psychological, and physical problems for the children (McGowan & Blumenthal 1978).

A Disturbing Trend

The number of women in state and federal prisons has nearly tripled during the past decade. In 1980, there were 12,331 women in our nation's prisons. By 1989, that number had grown to 40,566, an increase of 229 percent (BJS 1991). Approximately 87,000 women are currently incarcerated in U. S. jails and prisons.

Most women in U.S. prisons and jails are minorities. According to BJS, black women accounted for 46 percent and Hispanic women for 12 percent of the total

Barbara Bloom, M.S.W., is a nationally recognized expert on female offenders and their families. She is a consultant and researcher from Petaluma, California.

female prison population in 1986. Additionally, incarcerated women are young (twenty-five to twenty-nine years old), unmarried, poor, and undereducated with sporadic employment histories (ACA 1990; BJS 1991).

Most children of inmate mothers live with relatives, particularly maternal grandparents, during their mother's imprisonment. Some children, however, are placed in nonrelative foster homes and institutions. In certain cases, siblings may be separated by out-of-family placements.

A major impediment to the maintenance of mother-child relationships is that women's prisons are located in remote areas with little or no public transportation available. As a result, many inmate mothers receive few, if any, visits from their children. Distance from and lack of transportation to correctional facilities pose hardships for relative caregivers, many of whom do not have the financial resources to support frequent visitation. Additionally, many foster parents are reluctant to bring children to visit their mothers because of negatives feelings about the criminal behavior of the mother or views that prisons are no place for children.

Recent Studies of Female Offenders and Their Children

A 1978 study by the National Council on Crime and Delinquency (NCCD) offered a comprehensive and critical view of the nation's treatment of children whose mothers were incarcerated in U.S. jails and prisons (McGowan & Blumenthal 1978). It documented a neglected and forgotten class of young people whose lives were disrupted and often damaged by the experience of isolation from their imprisoned mothers.

The present NCCD study, released in January 1993, addresses the current issues and problems faced by incarcerated women, their children, and the children's caretakers. It also discusses the roles and responsibilities of correctional and child welfare agencies and offers an agenda for reform.

There are an estimated 1.5 million children of incarcerated parents in the United States (Center for Children of Incarcerated Parents 1992). Although no official data exist, NCCD conservatively estimates that on any given day in 1991, there were more than 167,000 children whose mothers were behind bars. Approximately three-fourths of all these children, or more than 125,000 children were under the age of eighteen.

The harm done to children by this experience can be sudden and substantial. There are immediate and sometimes long-lasting psychological effects. Peer relations and school performance may suffer, the mother-child relationship may be permanently damaged, and the child may be placed at greater risk of future incarceration by the criminal justice system.

A recent study by the Center for Children of Incarcerated Parents in Pasadena, California, found that more than 78 percent of the participants in its Therapeutic Intervention Project (TIP) had a parent who was previously or is currently in jail or prison. Recent studies estimate that the children of inmates are five to six times more likely than their peers to become incarcerated themselves (Barnhill and Dressel 1991).

Unfortunately, there continues to be a glaring lack of awareness and concern for these invisible victims. The punishment that these children suffer may not be intentional, but the effect is often the same. These children have unique problems and special needs. They are often traumatized by the arrest and imprisonment of their mothers. Additionally, in many cases, the forced separation from their mothers due to imprisonment is itself a cause of trauma to children (Bowlby 1980).

Results of the NCCD Study

Data for the NCCD study were gathered from questionnaires completed by 439 inmate mothers in jails and prisons located in California, Florida, Illinois, Minnesota, New York, Oklahoma, Pennsylvania, Texas, and Virginia (housing District of Columbia inmates).

Collectively, these respondents reported having 870 children under the age of eighteen. The questionnaires solicited information regarding the mother's background, children's background, mother-child relationship, and children's caretakers. Questionnaires were also completed by a limited number of caretakers of the children of incarcerated women, child welfare agencies, community-based providers, and correctional administrators. This information was supplemented by a series of face-to-face and/or telephone interviews with the mothers, correctional administrators, caretakers, and child welfare agency staff.

Profile of the Mothers

The women who participated in the study were in their early thirties, unmarried, and mothers of two or more children. Thirty-nine percent were African American, 34 percent were white, 16 percent were Hispanic, and 8 percent were Native American. A majority of the women did not complete high school, were unemployed, and had incomes below $10,000 per year. Forty-two percent received Aid to Families with Dependent Children (AFDC).

Nearly two-thirds of the women were incarcerated for nonviolent drug violations and property crimes. Approximately 40 percent of all women participating in the survey were incarcerated for a drug-related offense. The average number of prior incarcerations reported as an adult was 4.1. Sixty-five percent reported regular use of alcohol and/or other drugs. A disturbing 53 percent reported physical abuse, and 42 percent reported sexual abuse at some time in their lives.

Profile of the Children

Questionnaires completed by inmate mothers provided data for 870 children. The average number of children per mother was 2.6. The majority of children were under the age of ten, with an average age of 7.8 years. Gender of the children was 52 percent female and 48 percent male. African American children represented the largest percentage (43 percent), followed by white (24 percent), Hispanic (20 percent), and Native American (7 percent) children.

Although 73 percent of the incarcerated mothers reported that they had custody of their children at the time of arrest, only 67 percent stated that they lived with their children prior to incarceration. Only 58 percent of women in jail had custody of their children at the time of arrest, versus 76 percent of women in prison, and 55 percent stated that they lived with their children at the time of arrest, versus 70 percent of women in prison. This finding is consistent with a study of women in jail where 60 percent of the mothers reported that one or more of their children lived with them prior to arrest (Hairston 1991).

Profile of the Caregivers

Information about caregivers for children of incarcerated women has been limited, at best. For the most part, when a mother is convicted, her children are placed with relatives or friends. NCCD received completed surveys from thirty-five caregivers, reporting a total of sixty-six children of incarcerated mothers in their care. The data illustrate that the majority of children of incarcerated women were living with relatives (in 80 percent of the cases). Maternal grandmothers over fifty years old were the most frequent caretakers, followed by other relatives and the children's fathers. More than 7 percent of the children were in nonrelative foster care.

Of the nearly 9 percent of female inmates who gave birth while incarcerated, 67 percent stated that their infants went to live with relatives. A small percentage were placed in foster care (3.5 percent) or adopted (1.8 percent).

Relative caregivers experience both financial and emotional adjustments when they assume care for these children. Two-thirds of the caregivers reported that the amount of financial support they received was not enough to meet the necessary expenses of the child. They provided support for the children in their care primarily from Aid to Families with Dependent Children and their own personal incomes. Grandparents expressed difficulty in assuming the parenting role at a time in their lives when they had been looking forward to retirement. Some of the children in their care are experiencing emotional and health problems, which require stamina and resources that some grandparents feel unable to provide.

Perceptions of Children's Problems

A number of studies have documented that children of incarcerated parents suffer emotional stress related to the separation caused by a parent's imprisonment (Sack, Seidler & Thomas 1976; McGowan & Blumenthal 1978; Stanton 1980; Sametz 1980; Fishman 1982). They often exhibit behavior patterns that include anxiety, depression, aggression, and learning disorders. More recent research indicates some children of inmates may suffer from post-traumatic stress syndrome (Kampfner 1990).

Information about the children in this study was limited to responses received from inmate mothers and children's caregivers. The incarcerated mothers perceived that their children had problems primarily related to learning and school performance (18 percent of the children) and behavior (16 percent).

The children's caretakers tended to report higher levels of disturbance among the children than did the mothers. The caretakers reported problems among the children related to learning or school performance (29 percent of the children in their care) and behavior (27 percent).

The Center for Children of Incarcerated Parents (1992) reported that children of offenders are "by history and current behavior, the most likely among their peers to enter the criminal justice system." The study found that these children begin to demonstrate emotional reactions to the events of their lives at a very young age. Many express anger, defiance, irritability, and aggression. By preadolescence, these children express their reactive behavior in the classroom through disruption, poor performance, and truancy.

These data suggest that there may be three major factors that place these children at greater risk in comparison with their peers: they are traumatized by events relating to parental crime and arrest, they are more vulnerable as a result of separation from their parents, and they experience an inadequate quality of care due to extreme poverty.

Contact between Imprisoned Mothers and Their Children

Despite their concerns about maintaining contact with their children, the women in the NCCD study seldom saw their children while incarcerated. More than 54 percent of the mothers reported that their children had *never* visited them during their term of imprisonment. Seven percent received visits once a year or less, 12 percent received visits every four to six months, and 17 percent received visits once a month. Only 10 percent of the mothers reported receiving visits once or more per week.

Distance from the correctional facility was the main reason most often cited for lack of contact between the mothers and their children. Most respondents (62 percent) stated that their children lived more than 100 miles from the correctional facility. Forty-seven percent of the children of jailed mothers lived between 21 and 100 miles away from the facility.

Women in jails were visited more frequently than women in prisons (more visits of once or more per week). However, 60 percent of the women in jail *never* received visits from their children while incarcerated. Letters were the main form of contact between mothers and their children, followed by telephone calls and visits. In spite of the lack of contact with their children during incarceration, the majority of mothers planned to reestablish a home for all of their children on release.

The Role of Corrections

While there are some correctional institutions with model programs for female inmates and their families, many departments of correction have failed to develop adequate policies and programs for incarcerated mothers and their children. One-third of the mothers responding to the NCCD survey reported an absence of programs at the institutions where they were incarcerated. Issues that merit the attention of jail and prison administrators include the following:

- choice of placement for the inmate mother
- programs for pregnant inmates
- the nature and quality of permitted contacts between mothers and their children
- the development of services to enhance family unity on release

- cooperation with child welfare and other agencies that share responsibility for the inmate mother and her children

Most state correctional agencies have the discretion to select the place of incarceration. Depending on the laws of the state, this administrative choice may include the option of placement in a community corrections program. Community corrections programs are becoming a viable intermediate sanction for inmate mothers and mothers-to-be.

NCCD gathered information on community-based residential programs for incarcerated mothers in California, Massachusetts, Minnesota, North Carolina, Pennsylvania, Texas, Washington, and Wisconsin. Some of these programs only accept pregnant women; others serve women with young children and are more broadly focused on the maintenance of family ties and on successful community reentry.

While there are some excellent models of community-based alternatives to incarceration for pregnant women, such as Neil J. Houston House in Boston, and mothers of young children, such as the Community Prisoner Mother programs in California, these programs are too few and are only able to serve a small proportion of the women who meet their eligibility criteria.

There are community-based programs that work with correctional agencies in some states to facilitate prison visits and to provide family support services. For example, Aid to Imprisoned Mothers in Atlanta, Georgia, provides free transportation for family visits, as well as educational and recreational activities for the children of inmate mothers. Models based on California's Prison MATCH Children's Center program have been established at the Chillicothe Correctional Facility in Missouri, Topeka Correctional Facility in Kansas, and in Bexar County, Texas. These types of programs provide inmates with an opportunity to visit with their children in a "child-centered environment" that promotes positive interaction.

In general, correctional support programs for incarcerated mothers are scarce, falling short of the overall need. While most corrections agencies have a long way to go in meeting the fundamental needs of imprisoned women and their children, there are limits to the role of corrections. The courts and child welfare agencies have the primary responsibility for decisions affecting the mother's right to legal custody and the children's placement during her term of confinement and after her release. While the roles of the corrections and child welfare systems are separate, they also overlap to some degree.

The Role of Child Welfare Agencies

In theory, the children of incarcerated women would seem to be candidates for the benign intervention of child welfare workers delivering family reunification services prescribed by federal and state child welfare reform laws. In practice, the child welfare system, even as reformed, does not respond in any routine manner when a parent is incarcerated. Even when child welfare workers do intervene, their response may be unhelpful to the mother or to her children for a variety of reasons.

First, in the absence of a report of abuse or neglect, child welfare workers lack a jurisdictional or legal basis for intervention. This does not imply that these children are beyond the reach of the welfare system; they will become part of the local child welfare caseload if abandonment or neglect is reported. For example, if police officers notify the agency that shelter is needed for the children of an arrested mother, the children are eligible for processing into the welfare system as minors in need of supervision.

Most child welfare experts interviewed by NCCD cautioned against a requirement of routine notification. They noted that there may be little reason for child welfare agency intervention when the incarcerated mother has already made suitable arrangements for the care of her children. Additionally, the intervention of the public child welfare agency may actually work to the detriment of the incarcerated mother because she may lose legal custody of her children in court proceedings triggered by an investigation.

When the child welfare agency does assume jurisdiction of children whose mothers are imprisoned, it is required to make "reasonable efforts" to provide services that will promote family reunification. The need for reunification services may be especially great in cases where the children are placed in the custody of unrelated foster parents, because these caregivers may lack family and emotional ties to the mother.

Child welfare agencies have been criticized by some advocates and service providers for failure to deliver mandated reunification services to incarcerated mothers and their children. In some situations, where children are in foster care and the mother is incarcerated at a distance from her children, social workers may find it difficult to facilitate visits to the correctional facility. Social workers may, in some cases, believe that reunification services are unlikely to succeed, based on the mother's past behavior. A child welfare administrator for a large metropolitan city told NCCD that child welfare workers "traditionally view the parents as the source of the problem."

Even where the child welfare workers do provide reunification services to incarcerated mothers, those mothers may find it difficult to meet the legal requirements for reunification. For example, child welfare laws provide for termination of parental rights if the parent has failed to maintain an adequate relationship with a child who is in foster care. Imprisonment, by its very nature, poses serious obstacles to the maintenance of mother-child relationships.

Although legal and jurisdictional rules keep many children of inmate mothers out of the child welfare system, there is still much that the system can do once a case falls within its official purview. If the agency is making an initial placement decision, it can exercise the legal preference for placement of the children with extended family members. Another positive approach for child welfare agencies is to ensure that, once involved in the case, they have adequate support services to deliver. For example, the New York City Child Welfare Administration has developed a special program for incarcerated mothers and their children. Their Family Connectedness Program facilitates family visits in jail or prison with schedules that encourage maximum family participation. The child welfare workers pick up the children from foster homes and transport them to various New York correctional institutions.

Another way in which child welfare agencies can help in these cases is to acknowledge the needs of the caregivers of the children of incarcerated women. Kinship care programs, which qualify relative caregivers for foster care payments, are especially beneficial because they deliver higher levels of public support to caregivers in need of greater financial resources.

Finally, greater cooperation is needed between child welfare and corrections systems in cases involving incarcerated parents and their children. In particular, these agencies need to devise better mechanisms to coordinate prison and jail visits and to establish in-house correctional programs relating to parenting and family reunification.

Conclusion

If the rate of women's imprisonment continues to climb as it has during the past decade, increasing numbers of families will suffer. When mothers are incarcerated they do not automatically relinquish their parental roles, obligations, or concerns. Although they may be separated, they continue to care about the well-being of their children, and ultimately, most reunite with their families on release from jail or prison. Consequently, it is of vital importance to maintain the integrity of the family whenever possible.

The NCCD study represents one effort to broaden national awareness of the problems faced by incarcerated mothers and their children and to establish an agenda for reform. While it can help, no single study can provide ongoing momentum for change. Unless this issue is embraced by policy makers throughout the country and a reform agenda is implemented, the necessary changes will not occur. Our society cannot afford to continue to ignore the plight of the children of incarcerated women, because generations to come will suffer the consequences.

References

American Correctional Association. 1990. *The Female Offender: What does the future hold?* Laurel, Md.: American Correctional Association.

Baugh, C. 1985. *Women in jail and prison: A training manual for volunteers and advocates.* New York: National Council of Churches.

Barnhill, S., and P. Dressel. 1991. *Three Generations at Risk.* Atlanta, Ga.: Aid to Imprisoned Mothers. Unpublished.

Bloom, B., and D. Steinhart. 1993. *Why punish the children?: A reappraisal of the children of incarcerated mothers in America.* San Francisco: National Council on Crime and Delinquency.

Bloom, B. 1989. Mothers in prison: A neglected population. *Centerforce Journal* 18:7.

Bowlby, J. 1980. *Attachment and loss.* New York: Basic Books.

Bureau of Justice Statistics. 1991. *Special report on women in prison.* Washington D.C.: GPO.

Center for Children of Incarcerated Parents. 1992. *Report no. 6: Children of offenders.* Pasadena, Calif.: Pacific Oaks College and Children's Programs.

Datesman, S. K., and G. L. Cales. 1983. I'm still the same mommy: Maintaining the mother/child relationship in prison. *The Prison Journal* :143-54.

Fishman, S. H. 1982. The impact of incarceration on children of offenders. *Journal of Children in Contemporary Society* 15:89-99.

Hairston, C. F. 1991. Mothers in jail: Parent-child separation and jail visitation. *Affilia* 6 (2): 9-27.

Kampfner, C. J. 1990. *Post-traumatic stress disorder in the children that witnessed their mother's arrest.* Unpublished.

McGowan, B. G., and K. L. Blumenthal. 1978. *Why punish the children? A study of children of women prisoners.* Hackensack, N.J.: National Council on Crime and Delinquency.

Sack, W. H., J. Seider, and S. Thomas. 1976. The children of imprisoned parents: A psychosocial explanation. *American Journal of Orthopsychiatry* 46:618-28.

Sametz, L. 1980. Children of incarcerated women. *Social Work* 25:298-303.

Stanton, A. M. 1980. *When mothers go to jail.* Lexington, Mass.: Lexington Books.

XII.

The Unique Pastoral Needs of Incarcerated Women

by Sr. Susan M. VanBaalen, O.P.

Yesterday my brother
Came to say
My mother and my baby
Had went far away.

The poetic expression of an unknown incarcerated woman speaks volumes about the unique pastoral needs of the female offender. It speaks of her alienation from family, her loss of contact with her children, her lack of formal education, and her need to love and be loved.

Pastoral care of female offenders is even more complex than the language that describes it. The spiritual and religious needs of incarcerated women are as varied as their cultural and religious experiences, though issues and concerns expressed by women in a correctional setting will predictably match many of those chaplains face when providing ministry in the community. Perhaps women's needs are more intense and/or more pronounced in prison, but not more prevalent.

Women and men serve their sentences in very different ways. What has "always been" an acceptable accommodation for the needs of incarcerated men has fallen short of the needs of incarcerated women. Seemingly workable programming, housing, and custodial practices have provided less-than-ideal conditions of confinement for female inmates. In short, what has been effective for men doing time is not a viable framework for women in prison.

This chapter will focus primarily on the religious and spiritual needs of women in prison and explore the differences between men and women. It will examine the uniqueness and diversity of women's spirituality and the ways that a woman's integration (as well as her disintegration or her reintegration) centers in her spirit. It will provide a philosophical and theological grounding for the development of a unique style of pastoral care for women.

This chapter represents the work of a Bureau of Prisons National Chaplaincy Taskforce. Taskforce members include Rev. Kathryn Browder; Sr. Joan Campbell, S.P.; Rev. Angela Church; Rev. Donna Manning, Sr. Maryann Palko; Sr. Dorothy Rasche, S.P.; and Sr. Susan M. Van Baalen, O.P. All are chaplains in the Federal Bureau of Prisons.

Sr. Susan M. VanBaalen, O.P., is the regional chaplaincy administrator for the North Central Regional Office of the Federal Bureau of Prisons and is the main author of this work.

Relating to Others and God

There is an acute awareness and understanding of the differences between the sexes in rudimentary styles of understanding and relating to others and to God. The traditional patriarchal approach to spirituality has been one of authoritative hierarchy. This widespread belief system places the male image of God in ultimate authority, then man, with woman firmly set beneath the two in a pyramidal figure.

On the other hand, spirituality from a woman's worldview is more holistic, embracing a relationship with God and all creation. This manner of spirituality stems from a historical and cultural restriction of women and their gender roles in organized religion. Traditionally, the woman has been assigned a subservient position within her own belief system. This has generated both positive and negative results in her spirituality. In institutional church settings, the woman is most commonly relegated to lay ministry positions and not leadership roles. From subservience she has been able to bring great accomplishments to fruition. This accounts for a strong peer ministry of service among women, both in correctional settings and in the wider community.

The holism of women's spirituality dictates that one's religious experience is not limited to her experience of God and church, but that it also provides a framework for integrating all else that is good. Spirituality encompasses all of our relationships. This broadens and deepens the need for a unique pastoral approach to female offenders. An awareness of God and a commitment to God emerge from the acceptance, love, and respect of other believers.

The female inmate comes into the correctional setting with a complex self-understanding. First, she is a woman, which in and of itself has been less than acceptable throughout history. She is relegated to serving her sentence with other women whom she has been taught are, like herself, unworthy of attention. If there has been a dominant male in her life, he has more than likely severed ties with her along the way, leaving her emotionally, physically, and psychologically destitute as she faces incarceration and the accompanying alienation.

Traditionally, the woman's place has been with her family as mother and nurturer. Suddenly, incarceration deprives her of the caregiver role in which she finds both her identity and her fulfillment as a woman. She may experience an intense alienation because of both geographical and emotional distance from her family. Her inability to locate and communicate with dependent children is often devastating. Families move, children are placed in foster care or with distant relatives, and the woman is not notified. Telephone numbers change or are blocked, and contact is severed abruptly with the dreaded impersonal message of the operator, "I'm sorry, ma'am, that number is no longer in service" or "This party is no longer able to accept collect calls." The door is closed on the woman, caregiver, nurturer, provider...female inmate. Effective pastoral care requires that chaplains walk with female offenders on their spiritual journey from alienation and brokenness to a wholeness characterized by a healthy sense of self and healthy relationships with others.

The past ten years have witnessed the doubling of the number of incarcerated women. However, correctional policy, programming, and staffing patterns are not shaped for the minority. This reflects heavily on the conditions of confinement for women in jails and prisons. It places an added challenge on chaplains to ensure a pastoral presence and programming to compensate for the structures and programs developed for a predominantly male system.

For example, sound correctional practice requires that staff and inmate, even inmate and inmate, not develop a level of familiarity characterized by respectful touch of one another. While this distance is dictated by sound correctional judgment for the majority (men), experience indicates that it does not apply similarly to women's interaction with other women. Appropriate, dignified touch may contribute to a female inmate's sense of dignity and self-worth in a dramatically wholesome way. A woman whose adult experience of touch has generally been neutral or even worse, negative (assaultive, physically or sexually abusive, or chemically driven manipulation), responds to the warmth of another's genuinely respectful touch with grace, dignity, and a new sense of self.

Relationships and Family

The psychology of woman seems inseparable from her spirit, and the psychological dimension of her problems interfaces so closely with the spiritual that they become one and the same. Alone, she is insecure, frightened, and uncertain. She longs for the security of relationship and family.

Personal relationships help to define a woman's existence. Where there are none, the resiliency of her gender causes her to establish a relational place for herself, an emotional comfort zone. She begins by building a place of her own that reflects her character and personality. She then invites others into her space, and they become children and parents, sisters, and sometimes lovers.

A certain family-oriented interpersonal dynamic among women in prison is such a sociological phenomenon that scholarly books and articles have been written about it. It seems to occur in all women's prisons, but is not at all apparent in men's institutions. The family phenomenon is viewed by the casual male observer as unhealthy, even immoral. It is likened to lesbianism or aberrant sexual behavior, and at first glance, that is what it seems to be.

Yet a more respectful look reflects the need for women to be intimate, affectionate, and connected with one another in a way that men do not need or want. This is not to say that the "family" should go unchecked or unchallenged. The challenge must be an informed one, though, and offered out of a profound respect for the intimacy needs of women. This respect can shape a reverent understanding of the satisfaction derived from women's interrelatedness with one another as "family" members.

The "family" is not without its problems. The greatest of these is that they sometimes do lead to the same unhealthy dysfunctional relationships of dominance or sexual and emotional abuse that are found in many natural families. Although the need for family is great, the effect may well burden the members with unconscionable guilt, shame, fear, pain, and anger.

Relationships with men have often been devastating and have ended in a painful sense of loss. The "family," on the other hand, feels warm and comforting, secure and satisfying. "How could it be a sin?" is a question that is frequently asked of a chaplain by lonely women whose needs for intimacy are being met, but then stretched beyond their own acceptable limits. Limits on sexual behavior that are clearly articulated in prison regulations and moral codes that govern social interaction become albatrosses around the necks of women seeking intimacy in a system that disallows familiarity. A healthy need for intimacy becomes a painful, secret need for sexual gratification. If chaplains do not provide the accepting atmosphere for confronting this phenomenon, it is unlikely that the dilemma will be resolved.

Language

Women tend to think and speak in nondominating and noncompetitive patterns. An awareness of language patterns among women is an important clue to effective ministry to the spiritual needs of women. Women employ different language, as well as different images and symbols, to express the sacred. They may express their journey to wholeness as a journey home to self and God. When they express an interest in decorating the chapel, they are saying, "I need to create a holy space in which I can be at home with God." An expression of the need for a place of quiet or beauty reflects her personal longing for a dwelling place—a home where she is okay, where her relationship with God is transformed, and where her relationship with others is safe, acceptable, and one with her relationship with God.

Spirituality

Women first seek out an inner spiritual space characterized by quiet and beauty. The chapel, if there is one, becomes that sacred space where women can gather to be in the presence of God and one another in a healing and affirming way. It is a place where endless words of explanation need not account for her feeling of loss and alienation, a place where suspicion need not surround her feeble attempts to replicate a family of sorts. The chapel becomes a place to be alive in a lifeless environment. It becomes the place to dare to share, the place to risk one's story, the place to grow and change and become the woman she wants to be. It is a sacred space that opens itself to her grief and sorrow in times of loss and death. It is the place that nourishes her determination not to return to prison. It is the place that provides a new manner of relationship, one that does not manipulate, but is open and affirming instead. It is the place where women can offer up their deepest desires and be heard without recrimination. They can dream the dreams they have been denied and be affirmed by volunteers, chaplains, and one another.

The spirituality of women is often detectable in the quality of their interactions. The nurturing and sensitivity, the concern and commitment are all evidence of the uniqueness of relationships among women and the spiritual dimension they take on. Their gentle affection for one another is clearly lacking in healthy relationships among men and is viewed by most men as untoward, even abhorrent. The following story will clarify this difference.

A female inmate was told that her mother had died. The previous day she had tried unsuccessfully to reach her mother at the hospital. When the news came she was overcome with sorrow and guilt. In a daze she walked from her room and fell into the arms of an elderly woman who said no words, but opened her arms in comfort. The other women in the room encircled her. They reached out and touched her with compassion and caring. One woman, who spoke little English, was gesturing in an effort to understand. "Mama," said her roommate. "Mama," said the woman, beginning to weep with understanding. She walked to her bed and, clutching a rosary that lay on her pillow, sank to her knees and began to pray.

In another time and place, two hundred women gathered to memorialize and pray for a sister who had died of AIDS. Two hundred women who did not know her well, but who shared a deep sense of loss, a sadness over their sister's death in prison. It touches their own fear of dying in prison, their personal pain, and their own mortality and allows them to share this sense of alienation with one another in a healing way. The chaplain who enabled this cathartic event to occur touched the spirit of every lonely woman who lives with the fear of a similar experience of death. The fear and loneliness is diminished, though not taken away, by the community called "church" or "family" or "sisterhood."

The relational quality of women's spirituality is all-encompassing. It shelters the poor and the oppressed. It understands the wasteland of alienation and fear. It embraces the stranger with no home. Within these parameters, it offers a hope of wholeness. It reminds creation that each being was created with dignity and value. It presents an opportunity for women to be co-creators of all that is good and co-responsible for the generation of goodness. The opportunity to share in the creative process affirms the generativity of women and recognizes her as an equal partner in God's active design for harmony.

Pastoral Response to Women's Needs

The broader picture presents a framework from which to address the particular pastoral needs of incarcerated women. The following issues will receive primary attention in outlining a pastoral response: parenting, family, intimacy, self-esteem, and a sense of the sacred.

Parenting

Family issues and concerns probably consume the bulk of an incarcerated woman's psychic energy, emotional strength, and spirit. More than half the women in prison are mothers of dependent children. The incarcerated mother has often been the head of a single-parent household, and her situation immediately affects the quality of life of her uprooted children, to say nothing of the emotional and spiritual havoc it wreaks on the "fallen" mother. The need to connect with her children is often the reason for the first visit to the chapel for a female offender.

Long conversations with the chaplain, a sharing of pictures and pain, disappointments, and frustrations result in an easing of the stress but not of the pain, anger, guilt, shame, fear, and loneliness that a mother feels on abandoning or losing custody of her children through incarceration.

The sound of her child's voice strengthens and renews her spirit, giving focus to an otherwise meaningless existence. More frequent telephone contact between mothers and dependent children facilitated by pastoral care providers is a justifiable use of pastoral skills and resources. Children of incarcerated women are usually in foster care or are being cared for by already financially stretched family members, which makes collect calling unmanageable. Here is an instance where the sense of parity, rather than equal treatment between men and women, might shape the pastoral response. The need to connect with their children is one that expresses itself far more clearly and anxiously among female offenders.

Parenting classes, value clarification programs, and even role playing in preparation for visits with children prepare a female offender to assume her maternal caregiver role while incarcerated, as well as on her return to the community.

Maternal bonding is another critical family issue, particularly for incarcerated mothers who give birth while incarcerated or leave young infants at home when they are sentenced to prison. Often their previous lifestyle has prohibited mothers from developing the maternal qualities that result in bonding. Some incarcerated mothers need to be taught to touch with affection, hold, nurture, and love children appropriately.

Chaplains invest in the future of the family, the child, and the inmate when they become the mediators for bonding. One incarcerated mother of a newborn infant was encouraged by a chaplain to arrange to bring her infant's well-worn undershirt back to the prison with her on release from her maternity trip to the local hospital. For several months, the tiny shirt, holding the smells and memories of a beautiful infant, was the only link that mother had with her child. A smelly little shirt united the spirit of mother and infant until they could have a more suitable bonding experience.

Family Issues

Another concern for women in prison is simply the maintenance of ties with her own family of origin and/or her existing family support network in the community. While women family or extended family members in the community tend to maintain supportive contact with incarcerated men, the reverse is true for female offender's families. Random visitors' statistics bear this out.

A survey of the number of visitors and inmates visited on two Sundays in November 1991 at men's and women's prisons indicates a wide pattern of disparity. Combining the inmate populations at the Federal Medical Center, Rochester, Minnesota, and the United States Medical Center for Prisoners in Springfield, Missouri, provided the sample of men (1774), while the total number of inmates at the Federal Medical Center, Lexington, Kentucky, provided the women's sample (1720). The institutions are all administrative facilities, housing medical patient inmates as well as general population work cadres. On the randomly selected Sundays, seventy-two and seventy men were visited by 171 and 154 visitors, respectively. On those same two Sundays in November, thirty-six and twenty-eight women were visited by 116 and 60 visitors, respectively.

A more complete and scientific analysis would probably confirm the pattern suggested by this brief random sample. The evidence suggests that twice as many men benefit from the support of visitors as women in similar situations. It is not surprising, then, that some women tend to create a family to nurture and sustain them during their incarceration.

Visiting days are bittersweet times of great joy, excitement, anxiety, fear, and disappointment. Imagine the pain when one's child calls another "mommy" or understandably prefers to be held, fed, and loved by the foster caregiver rather than the natural incarcerated mother. Groups specifically designed to prepare a mother for visiting or to debrief after the visits offer a pastoral moment for growth, integration, and the gentlest of reality checks. Others who live with the same pain can provide a level of support that one-on-one ministry sometimes cannot provide.

Intimacy

Issues related to intimacy (incest, relationships, and sexual identity) will be considered together, as these are generally interrelated and are both a cause and a consequence of the family issues described. By the time a woman reaches early adulthood in a dysfunctional family, her boundaries have been violated so frequently as to distort her concept of intimacy. It is not uncommon to find that intimacy and sex are confused with each other. When this is the case, sex rather than intimacy is identified as the basic need. Coupled with the all-too-common residual effects of incest or other types of abuse, the outcome is frequently one of confusion and self-deprecation.

Incest Survival. An accepting and trusting environment provides the milieu for healing to take place and values to be clarified. The "unpacking" of the psyche is a slow and painful process that is not always understood or appreciated by those who have not been victims of abuse or who have repressed their own experience of it to survive. The prison chapel might be the only place where an incarcerated woman is secure enough to begin this dreadful journey.

What makes this experience so incomprehensible is the fact that victims will one day deny ever having been victimized and the next day recount terrible violations that could only have diminished her sense of self and her dignity. The memory of the abused tends to protect the victim from too full a recollection of her past until she is emotionally and spiritually able to live with its reality.

Part of the horror of incest and abuse is that the victim is, more often than not, perceived as the sinner or the seductress rather than an innocent victim. The shame and guilt that accompanies the victim's experience is a double victimization. Not only is she abused, but she also carries the accompanying shame and guilt, fear and loneliness, anger and pain with her into every new relationship.

Whether or not the fostering of this integrative process is a vital function of chaplaincy is debatable. Some would feel that this resides more logically under the purview of psychology. In some cases this is true, but in others, because of one's spiritual orientation and/or religious baggage, chaplaincy becomes the only place that is safe enough to delve into such a "sinful" experience. An ideal way to address the complex issues of incest and abuse would have components of both psychology and pastoral care in a holistic program designed to heal the spirit, wherein emotions reside.

Realistically, the locus of the program resides within the comfort zone of the victim. If she finds a climate for healing in the chapel, that is her healing place. If in psychology, that is the place. All too often, prison psychologists are so overwhelmed with intake screening and referrals for crisis intervention that these ever-present cases remain on the back burner to be addressed at a later date.

The process might be described as a moderated self-help process, best accomplished through group work and professional interventions. If particular chaplains feel inadequate to moderate such a healing group, professional pastoral counselors could be contracted to conduct the group and ritualize and celebrate the healing that occurs. With healing comes a healthier attitude toward all relationships, a sense of personal worth, and limits or boundaries that will not again be readily violated.

Relationships. The past relationships of women in prison seem to fall into three categories: unhealthy, unfinished, and broken. Unhealthy relationships include those of dependency, co-dependency, manipulation, subservience, or dominance. Self-help programs that advance personal and social awareness may result in movement from unhealthy to healthy, un-ease to ease in dealing with others in intimate or casual relationships. At the very least, she might become aware of her own patterns of relating and decide whether or not she chooses to change those patterns and move to a healthier attitude toward relationships.

Unfinished relationships include those that have been abruptly ended by abortion, relocation, abandonment, alienation, and death. In feeling and appearance, these are not unlike broken relationships characterized by separation or divorce, incarceration, or fractured family ties due to abuse, neglect, or failure to meet family conventions.

One of the more difficult aspects of dealing with anyone's unfinished relationships is that these often have to be brought to closure without the physical inclusion of the other party. Grief groups allow women to deal with the pain and anger, fear and loneliness, and shame and guilt of their losses. In a secure and safe environment characterized by love and acceptance, a woman is able to touch that core of her being where her loss is buried and forgive herself for what was unfelt, unspoken, or carelessly cast aside for the sake of the moment. She is able to "talk with" the person who is now absent from her life and tell them of her love, regrets, and sense of loss. She is able to forgive and experience forgiveness. She is able to finish her business.

Some broken relationships are permanently broken and are best dealt with as "unfinished," while others are fixable through counseling, group work, and programming that includes other parties to the relationship (parents, children, spouses, friends) who also long for wholeness in their relationships. Family seminars that include parents and/or children in an intergenerational setting might be patterned after the now generally accepted marriage seminar or marriage encounter.

Singular attention should be given to loss by abortion. Although a woman may deem abortion an acceptable method of birth control or termination of pregnancy, this is not without its own emotional consequence. Even though some women see no moral dilemma related to abortion, the residual pain and alienation often haunt her most private thoughts and feelings. A similar sense of emptiness and shame often accompanies a miscarriage. The mother questions whether her lifestyle, her subconscious rejection, or her carelessness with drugs and alcohol might have precipitated the loss of the fetus.

In either case, the loss is magnified by incarceration and separation from loved ones. Self-forgiveness only follows the assurance of love and forgiveness from God and the community. Chaplains frequently become the absolvers, the healers, the reconcilers who allow women to live with themselves and past decisions to terminate a pregnancy.

An important spiritual element to all relationship programming is the shared worship experience, the ritual celebration of the healing that has taken place within each person and among the relational units. Saying "I'm sorry" is not easy for most members of our society; it is even harder among those families fractured by abuse, crime, and all-too-glib apologies for the sake of a quick relational fix. Often it is only in a ritual setting that forgiveness is unconditionally offered and received by men and women whose lives and relationships have been broken by infidelity and alienation.

Sexual Identity.   Sexual identity is an issue that has to be dealt with in prisons, where large numbers of same-gender inmates are housed in close physical and psychic space. The absence of community and more conventional sexual partners often creates a sexual tension not experienced in a heterosexual environment.

Men and women seem to deal with this differently. If a man in prison meets his sexual needs through sexually acting out with another man, this is ordinarily done with the greatest of discretion. On the other hand, women tend to openly create family units to address their sexual needs as well as their need for community. It is not uncommon to observe female inmates affectionately touching each other, holding hands, or stroking one another's hair or body in a manner that at least suggests intimacy and may even be considered overtly sexual.

A woman who enters prison with a secure heterosexual identity often becomes confused by her own sexual attraction to other women. At first she is appalled by the behavior of others. Before too long, though, she may be repulsed and shamed by her own behavior. Still, she may continue to feel and act in a manner that she views as unacceptable. Young women sometimes come to believe that they are lesbians because they are physically attracted to other women while in a confined same-gender environment.

Pastoral concern warrants walking through this experience with a female inmate. It involves accepting her as she is so that she may grow and become the woman she wants to be. It involves a balance between affirming and challenging, thereby helping her to distinguish between one's needs for sex and for intimacy. Once a woman has distinguished between these needs, she is often able to discover healthier ways of having her needs for intimacy met. Only then she is able to begin a long-term fidelity to herself and her values. This process also benefits from a ritual experience of forgiveness and healing—not because the woman has sinned, but because her journey to wholeness has taken her through some painful and shameful experiences for which she feels the need of forgiveness and support.

Self-esteem

All of the previous issues contribute to poor self-esteem. Women who have been used and abused through unhealthy relationships, rape, incest, and physical abuse before incarceration come to the experience as wounded or broken women whose only image of self is enmeshed in others. The factors that have shaped this negative sense of self converge to destroy any self-worth. A ministry of quiet presence can help to affirm a woman's goodness and equip her to begin the journey to better self-esteem. The chaplain's affirmation, reality checks, and direction ease the struggle. Women derive a great benefit from individual and group opportunities to restructure their lives and reclaim their inherent goodness.

Because a woman in prison has a far greater need for community, she is often much more receptive to self-disclosure in a secure and comfortable group setting. Where a man might sometimes use this setting to secure his "macho" position in the group or on the compound, a woman is much more likely to openly share her woundedness and pain.

Volunteers provide a wonderful resource for development of self-worth. The opportunity to practice new behavior with people who will affirm, challenge, and love unconditionally is often the environment that nurtures growth and change. The essential value of volunteer programs is that they provide a nonthreatening arena for such encounters to occur. A woman's exegetical skill may well be the secondary outcome of a high-powered bible study. Its more critical outcome is the sense of dignity and self-worth that derives from quality interactions with good people. Healthy conversations with respected volunteers move inmates (both male and female) from self-absorption to social awareness. As they become more comfortable with others, they are rehearsing life as it can be for them when they re-enter the community.

The development of a healthy sense of self includes a process of unpacking as well as discovery. The painful letting go of past behavior, patterns of self-destruction, and memories of abuse and neglect must precede integration. Some women are able to use journaling or other creative expression to this end, but most need extensive personal and group work to let go and then to take charge of their own existence.

It is in spiritually oriented groups that a woman can be accepted for who she is right now, with a vision of who she can be in relation to God, self, and others. She begins to talk and learn group skills in a place where she feels safe. This security prepares her to carry herself with dignity as she moves into worlds that are less secure and familiar. A sense of empowerment begins to overcome the power of victimization. Empowerment allows a women to reclaim her dignity and self-worth by recognizing her own victimization by perpetrators who have robbed her of her sense of goodness and filled her with shame. The reshaping and molding of a personal ethic is clearly a sacrament of reconciliation that chaplains can proudly share with female offenders.

A Sense of the Sacred

Sacred space is perhaps more important to women than to men. Institutions that house women most often have to share space with another department or use the visiting room for worship. The common areas are often less private, less beautiful, and less accessible than a chapel would be. This limits the opportunities for a woman to claim a quiet time or space for herself. In circumstances where shared space is the norm, worship times are shaped by practical scheduling details rather than the most advantageous time for women to gather for prayer.

Not all women's institutions are able to provide a permanent, beautiful sacred space that is generally accessible to the women. Where men and women share common space, but at different times, the conventional sacred space is often not available to the women. The bulk of the programming time and space must be equitably apportioned to meet the needs of the predominantly male population, while the women gather for prayer or study in the same areas where they watch TV, play cards, or braid one another's hair. Pressing financial and labor constraints necessarily relegate construction and renovation of sacred space to a lower priority.

This situation places an added burden on the chaplain to create a sacred space out of the secular or even profane. Engendering a community called church sometimes softens the absence of space, but it does not take away the reality. The use of portable beauty is better than nothing. Such a void also offers women an opportunity to create something out of nothing. A scruffy old rug and a few bed sheets once transformed a corner of a prison gym into a sacred space! When women walked through the bedsheet-curtained wall and onto the carpet, their demeanors changed, their countenances softened, and there was an air of peace. The tearing down and rolling up of the chapel was always a sad ending to a rich and graced experience of shared faith, shared struggle, and sisterhood.

It is incumbent on the chaplain to create an environment of acceptance and peace. The ideal is that this spirit would be housed in a beautiful sacred space. The reality is that—at least for now—many women will continue to hunger for the place where God is, but will find God wherever people gather to encourage them to grow and change and become the women they long to be.

Conclusion

History has taught us that disruption, dissatisfaction, and litigation stem from a lack of awareness of diverse needs of individuals and groups who are different, to say nothing of the disrespect or irreverence for people that this incurs. Women and people of color should not have to adapt their values to those of the prevailing culture. Instead, they should have their values accepted as valid, and not deficient, though different. Women's religious experiences are intimately intertwined with those of men, yet lived out and expressed differently. This difference of faith experience and faith expression is what cries out for a unique response to the spiritual needs of incarcerated women.

XIII.

The Older Female Offender

by Joann B. Morton, D.P. A.

Being old, being female, or being an offender can all have negative implications in our society. Combined, they provide challenges for corrections now and in the future. Consider the following:

1. *"Annie," 72, a small, frail woman with scraggly white hair, crouches against the wall as a group of boisterous young women come down the hall. This is her first week in prison, and she is terrified. Everything is new. She is afraid that the fast-moving younger women will cause her to fall. She knows people at home who had suffered broken hips and were never the same. She is confused by all the noise and the instructions she has received; humiliated by the strip search and other intake processing; sore from trying to sleep on the thin prison mattress; and upset because she had trouble finding her room and was reprimanded by an officer. Above all, she has an overwhelming dread of dying in this stark, friendless place.*
2. *The warden reads the incident report and puts it down with a sigh. What are they going to do with "Mary"? Mary has been in and out of mental hospitals and prisons most of her adult life. She has a long history of assaultive behavior and at sixty shows no signs of mellowing. According to the report, this time she hit her roommate with her cane and threatened to kill the officer who intervened.*

These two cases illustrate the extremes correctional personnel face in dealing with older female offenders. They do not represent isolated instances. According to a recent study, women fifty years of age and older make up some 4 percent of the female inmates in this country (ACA 1990). In 1990, the number of women age fifty-five and older in state and federal prisons was fewer than 1,000 (ACA 1991), but the graying of the American population, as well as mandatory sentencing, harsh public attitudes, lack of community alternatives, increasing numbers of women being incarcerated, and the longer lifespan of women, will ensure that this number continues to grow. This chapter will review some relevant facts about aging and women, as well as factors to be considered in programming for incarcerated older women.

The population of the United States as a whole is becoming older, with those age sixty-five and older being the fastest growing age group (Feldman &

Joann B. Morton, D.P.A., is an associate professor in the College of Criminal Justice, University of South Carolina.

80

Humphrey 1989). By the year 2030 it is predicted that 65 million people will be age sixty-five and older.

One way to define aging is chronologically. Using years some define "older" as fifty-five and up; "elderly," sixty-five and older; "aged," seventy-five and older; and "very old," eighty-five and older (Lesnoff-Caravalia 1987). A 1992 study of administration issues relative to older inmates commissioned by the National Institute of Corrections recommended that for planning and programming purposes inmates should be considered "older" at fifty. While fifty is young by many standards, inmates generally have had lives that contribute to early aging and accompanying health problems that need to be addressed promptly in an institutional setting. An early start will help minimize some of the expense and hardship that a poor lifestyle creates. Prevention and health education programs should be implemented in all institutions housing older women. Chronological age is only one facet of aging, a process that can also be defined by the physical, emotional, social, and economic changes that come with advancing years. The rate at which these changes occur and how people cope with them are the result of complex interaction between heredity, lifestyle, socioeconomic conditions, and access to medical services (Yurick et al. 1984).

The bottom line is that older people are an extremely heterogeneous group with widely varying needs. Compare the level of functioning of your elderly relatives with other older people you know, and you will have some idea of the diversity among older people.

Older Women

Within the sixty-five-and-older age group the number of women is growing faster than the number of men (Kart, Metress & Metress 1988). Older women make up some 60 percent of older Americans; as age increases, the percentage of women in the general population also increases. Life expectancy for both caucasian women and minority women averages seven to eight years longer than men. Among minority populations, the gap between the longevity of men and women is widest among Native Americans (Lesnoff-Caravaglia 1987). Longevity does not, however, increase the quality of life. Older women often outlive their support system.

Consider the following facts comparing older women to older men:

1. Older women are more likely to live alone and have limited family support.
2. More older women—particularly minority women—live below the poverty level.
3. Older women often "fall through the cracks" of medical and financial support programs, as well as private insurance programs.
4. Older minority women are more likely to be ill and need medical care.
5. Older women make up three-fourths of all nursing home residents.
6. Older women have less hearing loss and less loss of taste, but higher incidents of certain debilitating diseases, including strokes, visual impairments, hypertension, and diabetes.

7. Osteoporosis, a degenerative bone condition affecting older women, causes them to be three to five times more likely to suffer from hip, back, and spine impairments.
8. Older women are portrayed more negatively than older men. They are seen as unattractive, ineffectual, unhealthy, asexual, and sedentary.
9. Middle-aged women find it more difficult to enter or reenter the workplace; they are viewed as "over the hill" more often than middle-aged men.
10. Although older women outnumber older men, most research on older people has focused on the effect of aging on men and ignored women. (Lesnoff-Caravaglia 1987; Kane, Evans & Macfadyen 1990; Yurick et al. 1984; Mummah & Smith 1981.)

Additionally, menopause, breast cancer (the prevalent malignancy among women) and hysterectomies can cause dramatic physical and psychological upheavals with which women must cope. Finally, many women need encouragement to take an active role in controlling their lives (AARP 1991). Keeping older women active and involved is critical in preventing dependency and helplessness.

Older Women in Prison

Both older offenders and female offenders are often referred to as "forgotten." Older women in prison are almost totally overlooked, even among the limited number of studies on female offenders.

Combining what is known about aging and older women with issues relevant to female offenders has serious implications for correctional programming. While the vast majority of older women are reasonably healthy, active people, lifestyle is a significant factor in how well one ages. Unfortunately, the lifestyle of many female offenders is not conducive to a viable old age. Incarceration also encourages dependency and passivity. There are some immediate programmatic implications that should be addressed relative to the incarcerated older female offender.

Staff selection and training are critical. Awareness of the medical and other needs of older women, as well as sensitivity when dealing with them, will help overcome some of the debilitating aspects of prison life for older women. All staff, particularly medical personnel, who work with this population should have training in gerontological health issues. Staffing patterns should also reflect that supervising older women is often more time consuming, for a variety of reasons, including visual and muscular impairments. Staff must also confront their own fears of aging and prejudices about older women. Not everyone can work effectively with this group.

Programming and supervision have to be individualized to meet the broad range of needs of this heterogeneous group. Individual program planning is particularly critical in prerelease preparation because the women's needs will vary, as will the resources in the community to which they return. It will be necessary in prerelease planning for older women to help with placement in residential facilities for the elderly or in nursing homes if needed.

Physical facilities will need to be designed or modified to accommodate a range of disabilities (this applies to men's institutions as well). Wheelchair access; color distinctions between floors, walls, and doorframes; comfortable places to sit; and handrails will aid those who have limited mobility. Older women need privacy and quiet space as much or more than younger women. Vulnerable older women, such as "Annie," will need protection from more predatory younger women.

The use of outside consultants and volunteers who have specialties in gerontology will greatly enhance the ability of correctional personnel to deal constructively with older women in prison, as well as assist their transition to the community. The network of service providers for the elderly, such as local councils on aging, can be invaluable when improving services for older women.

Creativity in modifying work and other activities to accommodate the interests, needs, and capabilities of older women will also be necessary. Work and other programs, which are not only critical to feelings of self-worth but also in many systems may provide time off of one's sentence for participation, must be accessible to the elderly.

Internal systems of rewards and punishments must be reevaluated in light of what is effective for older female offenders and their long-term well-being. The use of traditional lockups and loss of privileges may be counterproductive. Yet the "Marys" in this group must be handled as effectively as possible under the circumstances. Flexibility and creativity are essential.

Medical services should not only be gender-sensitive but be planned to meet the needs of older women. This includes special diets, as well as physical therapy, to counter osteoporosis and other potentially debilitating conditions. Regular mammograms, pap smears, and other diagnostic work should be offered in accordance with prevailing community standards. An ounce of prevention will have long-term benefits. Many older women are reluctant to assert themselves with medical staff or will simply agree with instructions received without clearly understanding what is happening. Staff must be aware that it is all too easy to attribute symptoms of illness to old age and ignore serious medical problems. Continuity of medical care on release will require additional effort. Liaisons with community health providers will ensure accessibility to medications and other services that some older women will need.

Issues of loss including death and dying also must be considered when working with this age group. Women will need legal assistance with matters such as wills and living wills, as well as spiritual guidance and solace. When a death does occur, it can be traumatic for both staff and other inmates who may have worked closely with the older woman. Counseling, crisis intervention, and closure in the form of a funeral or memorial service can be helpful.

Conclusion

The list above is only a beginning. Older female offenders, even in small numbers, pose many challenges for correctional personnel. Now is the time to start addressing them, as well as considering alternative sanctions or timely release of those who pose no threat to themselves or to the community. Acting now may avoid a costly correctional crisis in the future.

References

American Association of Retired Persons. 1991. Fighting for the rights of older women inmates. *AARP Highlights* (July/August): 1, 8.

American Correctional Association. 1990. *The female offender: What does the future hold?* Laurel, Md.: American Correctional Association.

American Correctional Association. 1991. *Directory of juvenile and adult correctional departments, institutions, agencies, and paroling authorities.* Laurel, Md.: American Correctional Association.

Feldman, R. H. L., and J. H. Humphrey. 1989. *Advances in health education: Current research*: 2. New York: AMS Press, Inc.

Kane, R. L., J. G. Evans, and D. Macfadyen, eds. 1990. *Improving the health of older people: A world view.* New York: Oxford University Press.

Kart, C. S., E. K. Metress, and S. P. Metress, 1988. *Aging, health, and society.* Boston: Jones and Bartlett.

Lesnoff-Caravaglia, C., ed. 1987. *Handbook of applied gerontology.* New York: Human Service Press, Inc.

Mummah, H. R., and E. M. Smith. 1981. *The geriatric assistant.* New York: Mc-Graw-Hill.

Yurick, A. G., et al. 1984. *The aged person and the nursing process.* 2d ed. Norwalk, Conn.: Appleton-Century-Crofts.

XIV.

Turning Up the Lights: Hospices in Women's Prisons

by Angela Church

"Turn up the lights....
I don't want to go home in the dark."
—Last words of O. Henry, American short story writer

On a Sunday morning it was announced in chapel services at the Federal Correctional Institution in Lexington, Kentucky, that a hospice group would be started. The Hispanic inmates, who sat off to the side with an interpreter, giggled nervously and looked at the chaplain as if she had said something a little off. Later that day, the interpreter stopped the chaplain in food service and said, "I want to apologize to you, chaplain. I translated something very wrong in the service this morning. I thought you told us there was going to be a hostage group started here."

Thus began the experiences of the hospice volunteer companions to terminally ill women incarcerated at Lexington. In a way the translation was not all **wrong**; the volunteers have become "captive" to the belief that no one should go home in the dark without the light of compassion. Five inmates and four community volunteers have committed their time and talents to meeting the needs of women who are dying in prison.

"We are not different," said Terry Green, hospice volunteer trainer, "from the group that met in living rooms fifteen years ago, when a small group of people gathered to talk about a special kind of caring for the dying. We are alike in many ways—mostly women, probably sitting in a circle, sharing a belief that people should be allowed to die with dignity...."

The hospice movement was started in 1967 by Dame Cicely Saunders when she opened the Saint Christopher's Hospice in London. The first hospice in the United States began in 1974 in New Haven, Connecticut. The movement has committed itself to providing support and care for people in the final stage of terminal disease—believing that, through personalized service and a caring community, patients and families can attain the necessary state of preparation for death.

In corrections, beyond the increases in the overall population, a number of factors have encouraged the development of hospice programs: the aging of the population, increased sentence lengths, and the growing number of inmates who

---

Angela Church is a chaplain at the Federal Correctional Institution, Lexington, Kentucky.

are medically at risk due to serious substance abuse, HIV infection, and other problems.

The Role of the Hospice Volunteer

The duties of hospice volunteers are varied. They commit to visiting the patient at least twice a week—more if needed. They are on call for emergency situations. They help by writing letters, reading, playing games, and listening. One volunteer gives manicures to help the patients feel better about their appearance. Another arranged to have a photograph taken so a patient could send it to her children. The volunteer helped the woman fix her appearance before the photographer arrived for her first picture in years.

Recently, one of the hospice patients, a young woman, celebrated a birthday. Her disease had left her childlike. She repeatedly told everyone her birthday was coming. The hospice volunteers planned a surprise party to which staff members from the hospital unit would be invited. Other inmates would play guitar and sing. The nursing staff kept the secret as the young woman went from one to the other asking, "Does anyone know about a party? Did you know my birthday is coming?" Finally the hour arrived. She was invited to visit another patient's room; while they talked, an area was decorated with banners and party favors made by the volunteers. When she was led into the room, her face reflected her joy as her lips moved to the words of "Happy Birthday" being sung by all.

When the volunteers met later to reflect on the celebration, they were moved by the knowledge that this might be this woman's last birthday celebration. "There was a feeling of happiness," said one volunteer, "and there was this insurmountable sadness too. She had a wonderful birthday, and I'm glad we had a part in making it special."

Hospice volunteers also provide support for patients who seem to have given up their hope. For example, a community volunteer noticed a sack of yarn by a patient's bed; she had ordered it to make a sweater for her husband. "It's no use now," she said, "I know I'm going to die, and it'll never be knitted." The volunteer asked if she could do it for her. The woman asked, "You would do that for me?" The two women put their heads together to choose the right kind of sweater. Much of the work was done by the volunteer in her home, but she often brought the pieces and sat in the woman's room knitting.

When the woman was taken to the local hospital outside the prison, she was close to death. The volunteer came to visit her one day and roused her. She pulled from a shopping bag a sweater of earth tones. "Finished!" she exclaimed as she touched the woman's arm. With labored breath the patient smiled and said, "Beautiful! Please send it to him and tell him I love him." After she died the sweater was sent with a note explaining how it was made. By return mail came thanks and a box full of yarn that might be used for others.

Distancing and Compassion

A special concern is that professionalism in the correctional setting and the "distancing" between staff and inmates that it implies, makes it difficult for staff to show the compassion they feel. Without a way to express these feelings, staff who have close, prolonged contact with dying inmates risk burnout.

It's necessary for hospice volunteers and staff alike to come to grips with their own mortality and feelings about death. They must learn to understand the stages of death and dying and develop their verbal and nonverbal communication skills and especially their listening skills.

When a patient would not leave her room, her hospice worker was called by the nursing staff. She lay depressed and saddened that her children were far away. Voicing the guilt so many mothers in prison feel, she wondered why should she leave her room when she had been such a failure as a mother. Her hospice companion was able to listen and respond; before the end of the visit they were walking hand-in-hand up and down the hospital corridor.

Sometimes, an inmate will be granted a compassionate release to spend her last days at home with her family. Maria was such a woman. The request for her release had been submitted, and she awaited a decision. As she waited, the hospice workers stood with her, her life sustained by oxygen tubes and the will to see her sister one last time. Volunteers were called repeatedly to sit by her side during the long nights; she would hallucinate and imagine herself home. The volunteers soothed her with the hope that soon she would be with her family.

The compassionate release was granted. A surge of hope caused Maria to draw inner strength. Her hair, makeup, and nails must be done, her sweatsuit must be pressed. The hospice workers leapt into action. There was joy in the preparation, but the workers also knew they were preparing Maria for her final journey. When the morning arrived, Maria, a wheelchair, portable oxygen, an entourage of hospice volunteers, and staff made their way to the sallyport door.

She made the flight to her homeland without incident. When the plane touched down she checked her appearance, then asked the nurse to remove the oxygen tubing. She walked unassisted into the arms of her family. Two months later she died peacefully at home. "When I watched her go through that sallyport door it was as if part of me went with her," said one of the inmate volunteers. "I had been given the great privilege of knowing a woman of strength and faith. Her life touched mine. The facts of compassion I shared with her are small compared to the lessons she taught me."

Conclusion

Death is never easy to deal with, and for those in prison it is even more difficult because of their isolation. The hospice group gives many women in prison an opportunity to say "goodbye" by means of a memorial service. On one occasion twenty white helium-filled balloons representing those who had died were suspended over the altar in the chapel. At the end of the service 150 women filed into a courtyard in the pouring rain and watched as the balloons were released. The wind and rain threatened to whip them to the ground, but the balloons began to rise higher and higher, until one woman cried, "Look, they're over the wall! They're free."

The seed of the hospice movement is taking root at the Federal Correctional Institution in Lexington. As it flourishes it ensures compassionate concern for women who may die in prison. It will call forth inmates and noninmates alike to volunteer. It will celebrate the life of these women and give them dignity as human beings. They will not die alone, but will be embraced by a group of caring individuals who bring a commitment to meeting the needs of others.

"I was scared at first," says one of the volunteers, "scared that I would say the wrong thing, do the wrong thing, act the wrong way. But now I look forward to being with these women. They teach me more about life than about death."

XV.

Management Issues for Female Inmates on Death Row

by Jennie Lancaster

One of the leading critical issues for correctional managers in this decade is the management of the growing death row population in the United States. Recent legal trends indicate that states may also anticipate an increase in the number of executions that may occur. Typically, these discussions are directed to the male prison death row population, yet there are forty-one women under the sentence of death in this country, according to the NAACP Legal Education and Defense Fund. In talking with a number of correctional administrators, they admit the presence of female inmates on death row has not received specific attention on policies, conditions of confinement, and other issues that are unique to the female population.

Traditionally, female inmate issues do not receive the same level of professional attention to their management needs as the much larger male population. This trend is changing as female populations dramatically increase, and the legal issues regarding parity are emerging. It is time to provide information to practitioners about female inmates on death row that can influence policy development, operational procedures, and the need for future agency planning for capital construction and program resources. The following areas should be reviewed on local and state levels.

Conditions of Confinement Issues

Housing

The number of female inmates under death sentences are small in comparison, and typically, may be one to three inmates at any given time. Currently, North Carolina houses the largest number of women in its death row, with six offenders assigned to this status. The typical housing configurations for women's facilities contain some type of segregation space, but these areas are designed to hold inmates who are restricted to cell time twenty-three hours daily. Consequently, the isolated death row inmate must endure similar restrictions, even though her behavior

Jennie Lancaster is female command manager for the North Carolina Department of Corrections Division of Prisons in Raleigh, North Carolina.

is acceptable. Many legal experts predict that these extremely restricted conditions will be challenged in the courts in the future.

The other option exercised by some states is to house the female death row inmate in the general population. This option can lead to several potential problems. First, typically the outside security perimeter is designed for medium custody security practices. A death row inmate could become a genuine escape risk as the various legal processes continue on the case. One could argue that a death row inmate might become more of an escape risk due to the ultimate penalty she faces. The notoriety of these cases would capture the immediate attention and scrutiny of the public and government officials. Typically, male inmates in the general population are housed inside a maximum custody facility with a secure perimeter; they are housed in one cellblock after they complete work and program assignments during the day.

The second potential problem with housing female death row inmates in the general population relates to the needs most inmates have to develop relationships and close emotional bonds. These women identify with each other and express feelings in a verbal and physical manner. In 1984, in the months preceding Velma Barfield's execution date in North Carolina, many inmates in the population began to seek staff assistance to manage their complex feelings related to her impending death. These inmates had gotten to know Barfield when they were housed in the segregation unit where she was housed the entire time. I had many conversations with these inmates and saw that they personalized her death. We developed strategies to work with these women and the rest of the population. These circumstances probably could have been far more problematic if Barfield had been housed in the general population. We made some structural changes in the segregation unit to provide her with significant out-of-cell time, but it was still inadequate.

North Carolina will soon begin construction on a new forty-eight single-cell maximum housing unit that will have a separate pod of eight cells, a dayroom, an activity room, a visiting area, and other specific design features applicable to the death row population. The housing dilemma for female death row inmates will predictably increase and should be addressed by correctional agencies in capital construction and renovation planning for women's facilities.

Medical/Mental Health Issues

The average age of female inmates is thirty. One could predict (and statistics support this) that these women enter prison with health problems that will be exacerbated by the effects of incarceration. A woman facing a period of lengthy incarceration encounters a variety of chronic health problems and diseases. These health problems include heart disease, hypertension, diabetes, seizure disorder, and the expected gynecological dysfunctions that can lead to surgery. Female offenders also frequent sick call in large numbers.

Understanding these basic medical issues for women, it should be expected that death row inmates will experience similar problems, requiring routine, and periodically, more lengthy treatments by medical staff. Security issues related to moving this status of offender can cause significant operational problems for a unit. A majority of women's facilities do not have secure areas to provide medical inpatient housing for death row inmates. Additionally, the typical segregated housing unit does not provide for adequate space for sick call triage or examinations to be conducted in a private and confidential manner. This is not a generic problem for transient inmates who may gain greater access to health services while in the population. Death row inmates spend years in this status, and provisions need to be made to address these medical problems in a legally defensible manner.

Many of these same problems can be echoed for the mental health needs of this population. These women display many of the expected characteristics of a female offender. Issues of abuse, substance abuse, dysfunctional relationships, and emotionally dependant personalities do appear in these women. The stress related to receiving the death penalty, and the isolation that this status can bring, can aggravate their own issues. It is important to offer routine access to a mental health professional for these women. Once a death row population grows to three, it also becomes important to provide group work for the women who are forced to live together with no involvement with other inmates. Living tensions and natural jealousies occur among the women as their own sentences weave through the system.

Additionally, the need to provide mental health inpatient treatment service to these women is very important, yet is almost nonexistent at women's prisons. The future capital planning for women's prison facilities should include the need to provide mental health services to all inmates in a reasonable manner that would be responsive to the population demographics of each locality.

Visitation

In most women's facilities in the country, female inmates are allowed to have contact visitation privileges. The primary principle for this tradition is the need to facilitate positive interaction between inmate mothers and their children. National data are consistent in reporting that 76 percent of female inmates are mothers (BJS 1991). Women on death row can have children in all ranges of age. It should also be recognized that the children can experience an extended sense of stress by nature of their mother's sentence and the expected lengthy number of years that the children may be required to visit at the unit. Jurisdictions should consider planning a visitation area that includes a small play area for children of special population inmates who have restricted visiting privileges. Another reason for mental health/social work intervention with death row women is to facilitate the parenting work for the inmates that becomes so stressful. Their children are subjected to a media replay of their crimes and trials every time a major appellate court decision is rendered in their case.

Another important issue for female inmates and their families is the need to maintain consistent communication. Typically, women's prisons are located far from urban areas and are not convenient to public transportation, thus precluding routine visitation by children. Death row inmates should be allowed phone privileges to contact their families and attorneys. There is no research to support that this phone communication is any type of security problem more significant for this population than for general population female offenders.

Program Services

One of the critical services for female death row inmates is chaplaincy. It is important to establish consistent access to the chaplain for these women. As the time on death row lengthens, the role of the chaplain becomes more of a stabilizing factor to the inmates and their families. The chaplain also can select quality volunteers to provide services and support for these women. Again, staff should seek support and venues for communication as a key way of managing female inmates. This support system needs to be constant and stable.

As far as traditional ideas about programming are concerned, it is understood that access to programs is severely limited for the segregated inmate, but some allowance needs to be made to provide access to educational programs and self-help materials. It is also desirable to provide some access to a type of meaningful job in the death row housing area. North Carolina is pursuing a bulk mail operation for another state agency as a work opportunity for the death row inmates.

Recreation needs for these women also vary from a more physically active male population, yet they request some type of exercise equipment to be available to them. Routinely these women request arts and crafts materials and need good lighting to make their crafts and to read. North Carolina has experimented with a biofeedback process for women with some reasonable success and interest; the mental health staff directed this training. Mental health staff need to be consulted about positive leisure-time activities for these women.

Execution Planning

Velma Barfield was executed 2 November 1984 in Raleigh, North Carolina, at Central Prison. There have not been any other executions of women since then, and she was the first woman to be executed in the United States in twenty-two years. As the superintendent of that women's prison, I learned that correctional agencies had not prepared for this type of situation.

If correctional agencies house women on death row, they should plan for the potential reality that inmates may actually be executed. The planning needs to be specific on issues about the inmate's management at the women's facility in the months/weeks prior to a realistic execution date, as well as the issues that need to be addressed at the men's institution that houses the death watch area/execution chamber. Some key elements of the general planning process are as follows:

1. Interagency planning should take place with key management staff of both prisons and the agency.
2. Interagency planning should include the attorney general, staff from the Governor's office, the DOC, and any other support agencies.
3. Media and public information management needs to be planned.
4. Staff preparation and training should include post-trauma support.
5. The relationship with the inmate lawyer(s) is a point of intense work for both wardens.
6. The relationship with the inmate's family must be a primary focus for both wardens.
7. Actual planning of the execution process needs to review any issues specific to managing a woman (i.e., execution clothing, death watch).
8. The staff and inmate population at the women's prison need planned attention to their response to this emotional event. I found my staff in 1984 to be highly committed and professional, and yet, they

confronted a dilemma for themselves in reexamining their mission as correctional caretakers. The medical and mental health staff faced their own ethical dilemmas about their specific roles.

The following are inmate issues that need to be addressed:

1. Family support, visits, and communication become important.
2. Grief preparation needs to include planning for a funeral, a will, organ donations, choice of execution methods, disposition of personal property, and other issues specific to that woman. It is important to limit key staff relating to the inmate, and the warden will become the main person making the decisions for the inmate and her family.
3. Unusual requests may be made by the inmate in the last several weeks to include media access, special religious rites, letters to other inmates and victims, special visits, and a variety of other issues that may arise.
4. It must be understood that many death row inmates consider the women's prison to be home, and she is confident and comfortable with the staff in this emotionally charged time. The timing of her movement to another prison for death watch needs careful consideration and planning by top agency managers.
5. During the period of death watch, the question of access to the inmate by treatment staff (chaplain, mental health, medical) from the women's prison needs to be addressed, because the inmate will likely request access to them during these days.

Conclusion

The issue of managing women on death row is new on the correctional agenda, and we are breaking new ground in our policy development in this area. In 1993, the National Institute of Corrections is offering, for the first time, a training seminar for managing death row populations/executions. A section of this seminar will address the unique problems concerning female inmates on death row. Dialogue needs to occur among managers in different states to gain new ideas and to share practical experience specific to female offenders on death row. It remains a critical correctional policy challenge for this decade.

Reference

Bureau of Justice Statistics. 1991. *Special report on women in prison.* Washington, D.C.: GPO.

XVI.

Sentencing Alternatives for Female Offenders

by Elizabeth Von Cleve, Ph.D., and Joseph G. Weis, Ph.D.

Historically, female offenders from different geographical areas have been housed together in one facility. That practice has made going to prison more punitive in some ways for women than men because the women have been separated more completely from their sources of support, especially their families (Daly 1989). It has also resulted in the commingling of violent and nonviolent, first-time and repeat, short-term and long-term, and mentally ill and normal offenders. Consequently, many female offenders, perhaps the majority, have been subjected to unnecessarily high security and inadequate programming because of the presence of some more serious and violent offenders (Stringer 1987). The overall result is insufficient attention to the needs of individual female offenders (Goetting 1985).

Sentencing Practices for Female Offenders

As a correctional management tool, the classification of offenders by individual characteristics and needs is intended to balance the rights of offenders to the minimum necessary restrictions against society's right to be protected. Nesbitt (1988) argues that effective classification mandates options that cannot be accomplished with a single institution and few alternatives to incarceration.

The deficiency of sentencing alternatives for juvenile female offenders may be the most serious problem confronting our juvenile justice system. There are fewer alternatives to institutionalization for girl delinquents than for boys, and girls are less likely to be placed in existing alternative programs, such as group homes or nonresidential day-treatment programs (Benedek 1979). The practice of using the most, rather than the least, restrictive placement early in a female offender's involvement in crime may reinforce patterns of criminality (Schur 1984).

Several corrections practitioners and researchers are now encouraging the increased use of community-based sentencing alternatives for both juvenile and adult female offenders (Chapman 1980; Goetting 1985; Haffner 1986; Im-

Elizabeth Von Cleve, Ph.D., is a lecturer, Society and Justice Program, at the University of Washington in Seattle.

Joseph G. Weis, Ph.D., is the director of the Center for Law and Justice and professor of sociology at the University of Washington in Seattle.

marigeon 1989; MacKenzie, Robinson & Campbell 1989; Rafter 1989). There are few reasons to keep female offenders who are not serious, violent, or repeat offenders in high-security institutions, and there are many reasons not to. Although imprisonment usually costs more than alternatives, separates children from their mothers, may contribute to career criminality by "teaching" crime, and is not primarily a rehabilitative experience, these facts are not weighed heavily in the sentencing decisions of courts and correctional systems for female offenders (Immarigeon 1989; Stringer 1987).

Corrections officials in Delaware authorized a study to estimate how many of the state's female inmates were appropriate candidates for alternative sanctions. Interviews with 93 percent of the female institutional population led to the conclusion that a "sizable percentage" qualified for alternative placement and "didn't need to be [incarcerated]" (Immarigeon 1989). Despite these and other studies that have reached similar conclusions, a majority of women serve their sentences in confinement.

Carlen (1985) and other British criminologists have offered explanations for the existence of this sentencing practice in their country. Carlen suggests that "the majority of female offenders are being sent to prison not because of the seriousness of their offenses, but because of the persistence of their nuisance." Women who are characterized by noncompliant behavior, homelessness, single or separated marital status, and alcohol or drug problems are more likely than "conventional" female offenders to go to prison (Farrington & Morris 1983; Worral 1981; Carlen 1983). In England, women are sent to prison because of their unstable home lives and the failure of social institutions to provide solutions to their problems (Smith 1984).

Those explanations, particularly the assertion that a woman's failure to meet "socially conditioned female gender-stereotype requirements" contributes to the likelihood of imprisonment rather than a less-punitive alternative, apply to female offenders in the United States as well (Carlen 1985). A comparative study of judicial processing and sentencing decisions in New York and Seattle shows that conventional "familied" women were treated more leniently than either men or nonfamilied women (Daly 1989). Data from Maryland also indicate that women in prison are more likely than those in community-based programs to have less formal education and a history of substance abuse and mental-health intervention and to have been unemployed at the time of their current offense (Immarigeon 1989).

In addition to parity issues, there are two compelling arguments for the increased use of sentencing alternatives for female offenders: to reduce the crowding in women's prisons and to preserve and strengthen offenders' families.

Reducing Crowding

Women have consistently made up about 4 percent of the incarcerated population in the United States. However, the absolute number of institutionalized women has been rising steadily since the late 1970s, without a concomitant increase in the number of prison beds (Barry 1985). The result is obvious: serious crowding in women's institutions in many states. Proposed solutions range from increasing bed space and building new prisons to expanded use of sentencing alternatives. The latter has been supported, particularly for nonviolent offenders, because it is recognized that reducing the prison population at the front end is more effective than doing so on release (Immarigeon 1989). This conclusion is buttressed by a study in Illinois of electronic home detention and intensive supervision probation and found that these community-based alternatives resulted in lower levels of recidivism among female offenders (Citizens Council on Women 1986). Of course, institutional programs cannot be improved until the crowding problem is addressed. Ironically, resolving the problem of crowding by increasing the number of offenders who receive alternative sentences should improve the services provided to both those in prison and those who are placed in the community.

Strengthening Families

Some argue that the benefits to society for imprisoning the mother outweigh the costs to her children. On the other hand, incarceration, particularly of women who are mothers, has been shown to accelerate the destruction of the family and perpetuate the cycle of poverty and crime (Haffner 1986). Incarceration without the possibility of maintaining family ties may even lead to the termination of a mother's custody rights, a punishment rarely experienced by male offenders and perhaps considerably harsher than intended by the courts. Fortunately, sentencing options exist that allow the court to punish the offender with minimal negative, and even some potentially positive, effects on her family.

Sentencing Options

Until the late 1970s, most of the community-based alternatives to incarceration were provided for male offenders, and those designated for women were modeled after male programs (Bershad 1985; Herbert 1985). The following are the sentencing options currently available for female offenders, from least to most restrictive:

Home-based, noninstitutional options
  Restitution
  Community service/volunteer work-service programs
  Probation
  Home detention/house arrest/electronic monitoring
  Intensive probation supervision
  Day treatment/community center nonresidential programs
  Home detention combined with intensive probation supervision

Community-based incarceration
  Community-based work release
  Community-based educational release

Community-center residential program
Private contractor residential program

Institutional incarceration
  Prison camps
  Work camps
  Cocorrectional facilities
  Institution-based work release
  Medium/maximum security women's facilities

Home-based Options

Several sentencing alternatives do not include serving time in a prison or residential facility. Restitution and community-service/voluntary work-service programs require payment in time or money for the crime committed. These programs can be combined with probation or home detention in the form of electronic monitoring and house arrest. Home-based programs provide supervision and increase the offenders' levels of accountability because the offenders bear the cost of participation. The cost of an alternative program is not always less than that of incarceration, although it is difficult to compare relative costs because of the possible indirect or unknown costs of both approaches, such as welfare and foster-care payments or the economic and social costs of recidivism (Stringer 1987).

Home detention is not appropriate for all types of offenders—it is particularly not suitable for career and violent criminals. Some research, such as the Illinois comparison of imprisonment and electronic home detention, have concluded that home-based programs also may not be appropriate for pregnant offenders or mothers because their home lives may be turbulent, and these women typically require more health and support services than they or the community can provide (Immarigeon 1989). However, the argument that offenders who are pregnant and/or mothers receive better services while they are in prison has not been consistently supported by the evidence (Greenspan 1988). That view also does not consider the potential effectiveness of noncorrectional community-based social services combined with noninstitutional sentences.

Increased levels of monitoring are possible through intensive probation supervision, the most cost-effective option identified in a recent study of community-based correctional alternatives (Citizens Council on Women 1987). Intensive probation supervision can be combined with home detention to provide a high degree of surveillance and supervision.

Day treatment programs, such as Genesis II for Women in Minnesota, offer nonresidential services for female offenders and their children who are referred by the court. The Guilford County Women's Residential/Day Center started as a residential facility, then added a day treatment component to provide structure and support during the day while the offender was allowed to return home to her children and family in the evening (Stringer 1987). Day treatment is sometimes offered through community centers that have been identified as a "natural service outlet" for offenders and their families (Jorgensen, Hernandez & Warren 1986). In general, home-based sentencing alternatives provide an appropriate level of supervision and support and, at the same time, cause the least amount of disruption to the family.

Community-based Incarceration

Community-based residential programs that include work and education release have been largely ignored as sentencing alternatives for women. This is particularly puzzling and disappointing in light of reviews by experts who have found community-based programs, such as the Elizabeth Fry Center in San Francisco, the Arizona Center for Women work-release program in Phoenix, and the Expectant Mothers Residence in Boston, to be the most promising rehabilitative programs for women (Ryan 1984; Immarigeon 1989; Stringer 1987). Community-based residential programs, whether operated by the government or private contractors, can serve as transition points between prison and the community or simply as alternatives to incarceration. Unfortunately, because of the small number of participants and the absence of evaluation studies, little is known about the effectiveness of these programs.

Although one of the purposes of community-based residential programs is to keep mothers and children together, only two of nineteen mother-child facilities examined in a 1983 study actually had children in residence (Neto & Bainer 1983). The problems associated with housing female offenders and their children in the community appear to require more attention and resolution by correctional administrators. Community-based residential programs must be recognized as worthwhile correctional endeavors that have been implemented successfully in many jurisdictions. For example, the Elizabeth Fry Center, a model program providing a comprehensive range of services for low-risk female offenders and their children up to six years old, has been in operation as a reentry program since 1986 (Immarigeon 1989; Stringer 1987). This program could serve as a model for the creation of similar facilities for female offenders in other jurisdictions.

Institutional Alternatives

Many women in prison do not have access to the institutional alternatives normally available to males, such as prison camps, work camps, or work release. The most popular institution-based alternative for women is the co-correctional facility that can be a prison, camp, or minimum security facility. Ironically, co-correctional programs may have some detrimental effects on the families of female offenders.

The Citizens Council on Women (1987) conducted an extensive assessment of co-correctional programs and discovered that while this type of alternative appears to offer a solution to the disparity between services available for male and female offenders, the outcomes are not always favorable. In Illinois, women were moved into a previously all-male institution to relieve crowding in the only state facility for women. Unfortunately, because only 9 percent of the population of the new co-correctional facility were women, fewer opportunities and services were available there than at the women's prison. Other problems included the need for increased monitoring and supervision of inmate movement, inadequate staffing levels, and increased expenses. In addition, the inmates who had more restrictions imposed on them, the staff who had to closely monitor male-female contacts and sexual behavior, and families of inmates who were threatened by inmates' increased interaction with members of the opposite sex, all experienced greater tension and stress. Illinois reported at least seven pregnancies attributable to interinmate sexual contacts during the first year of operation of the facility, which raised issues of paternity, financial responsibility for the children, placement of the children after birth, impact on other children or spouses, and appropriate sanctions for the offenders. Finally, the fear of pregnancy, coupled with a disproportionate ratio of men to women in a closed environment, may further perpetuate the dependent role already imposed on women within the criminal justice system and in the free world.

The assessment by the Citizens Council on Women also included a survey of thirty-five state and federal co-correctional programs and made the following recommendations, attributed to the warden of Wisconsin's only women's prison: Never establish a co-correctional facility where one sex far outnumbers the other at a jurisdiction's only women's facility, unless there is a clear programmatic rationale that it will be substantially more beneficial for both male and female participants. If a separate, truly co-correctional facility is not feasible, a more easily implemented variation is the shared facility, such as the Meadow Creek Correctional Center in Alaska, where men and women share programs and common space, but have completely separate living quarters, staffs, and administrations (Ryan 1984).

Conclusion

Corrections professionals should encourage the increased use of sentencing alternatives for female offenders. Many female offenders are mothers, and incarceration can lead to termination of custody rights, a punishment rarely experienced by men and one that is considerably harsher than intended. Sentencing alternatives can preserve female offenders' families and reduce institutional crowding. Noninstitutional options can be either home-based (restitution, intensive probation, home detention) or community-based (work release, day treatment). These alternatives can be used with minimal risk to the community and potentially positive effects on the female offender and her family.

References

Barry, E. 1985. Reunification difficult for incarcerated parents and their children. *Youth Law News*:14-16.

Benedek, E. 1979. Female delinquency: Fantasies, facts, and future. *Adolescent Psychiatry* 7:524-39.

Bershad, L. 1985. Discriminatory treatment of the female offender in criminal justice. *Boston College Law Review* 26:389-438.

Carlen, P. 1983. *Women's imprisonment.* London: Routledge and Kegan-Paul.

———. 1985. Law, psychiatry, and women's imprisonment: A sociological view. *British Journal of Psychiatry* 146:618-21.

Chapman, J. 1980. *Criminal justice programs for women offenders.* Washington, D.C.: Center for Women Policy Studies.

Citizens Council on Women. 1986. *Annual report.* Springfield, Illinois: Citizens Assembly, Illinois General Assembly.

Citizens Council on Women. 1987. *Annual report.* Springfield, Illinois: Citizens Assembly, Illinois General Assembly.

Daly, K. 1989. Neither conflict nor labeling nor paternalism will suffice: Intersections of race, ethnicity, gender, and family in criminal court decisions. *Crime and Delinquency* 35:136-68.

Farrington, D., and A. Morris. 1983. Sex, sentencing, and reconviction. *British Journal of Criminology* 23:229-48.

Goetting, A. 1985. Racism, sexism, and ageism in the prison community. *Federal Probation* 49:10-22.

Greenspan, J. 1988. Minnesota's newest prison provides humane environment. *Journal of the National Prison Project* 17:16-19.

Haffner, D. 1986. *The Elizabeth Fry Center.* San Francisco: Council of Churches.

Herbert, R. 1985. Women's prisons: An equal protection evaluation. *The Yale Law Journal* 94:1182-206.

Immarigeon, K. 1989. Four states study policies affecting women offenders. *Journal of the National Prison Project* 19:4-6.

Jorgensen, J., S. Hernandez, and R. Warren. 1986. Addressing the social needs of families of prisoners: A tool for inmate rehabilitation. *Federal Probation* 50:47-52.

MacKenzie, D., J. Robinson, and C. Campbell. 1989. Long-term incarceration of female offenders: Prison adjustment and coping. *Criminal Justice and Behavior* 16:223-38.

Nesbitt, C. 1988. Creativity in programming for female offenders. In *Proceedings of the 117th Annual Congress of the American Correctional Association.* College Park, Md.: American Correctional Association.

Neto, V., and L. Bainer. 1983. Mother and wife locked up: A day with the family. *The Prison Journal* 63:124-40.

Rafter, N. 1989. *The American prison: issues in research and policy.* New York: Plenum.

Ryan, T. 1984. *State-of the art analysis of adult female offenders and institutional programs.* Boulder, Colo.: National Institute of Corrections.

Schur, E. 1984. *Labeling women deviant: Gender, stigma, and social control.* New York: Random House.

Smith, R. 1984. Women in prison. *British Medical Journal* 288:630-33.

Stringer, T. 1987. *Sentencing alternatives for Illinois female offenders.* Springfield, Ill.: Administrative Office of the Illinois Courts.

Worral, A. 1981. Out of place: Female offenders in court. *Probation Journal* 28:90-93.

XVII.

The 5-South Unit at MCC New York

by Marcia Baruch

Surrounded by Chinatown, Little Italy, taxicabs, and people traveling back and forth to work is a building hidden in the heart of downtown Manhattan. Those who hurriedly walk past see just another co-op—pleasant in appearance with good security. Few are aware that the officers patrolling are not protecting the tenants of an apartment building but are guarding one of the Federal Bureau of Prisons' "high-rise" detention centers—the New York Metropolitan Correctional Center (MCC New York).

About 900 inmates, most of them awaiting trial, live in this building in nine separate housing units—each with its own personality and problems. One of these units is more likely to produce shivers in officers when they are given it as a new assignment. It's not the segregation unit or a unit housing the most dangerous offenders. It's 5-South, a unit with about 120 women—the only women's housing unit at MCC New York. During a recent roll call I observed an officer as he was informed that he would be working at 5-South. He handled the news eloquently; he rolled his eyes, put his head down on the table, and groaned to no one in particular, "Oh no!"

Why is 5-South considered to be one of the most difficult units to work on, or just to walk on? We might be able to answer that question by answering this one: What is it like to be a female incarcerated at MCC New York?

Female Inmate versus Male Inmate Concerns

A typical day for an inmate on the unit is to wake up, dress, eat, and remain on the unit. Since there is an understandable concern regarding male and female inmates mingling in the prison, the majority rules—male inmates have the privilege of leaving their unit with a pass or reporting to a daily work detail, while female inmates must be escorted, and their movement is limited. While male inmates can be transferred to another facility at Otisville, New York, which offers more activities, female inmates must remain at MCC New York until they are sentenced. This leads to greater restlessness, agitation, and depression. Some say by nature women

Marcia Baruch is the chief psychologist at the Metropolitan Correctional Center, New York.

show their emotions more than men—just as it is okay for them to cry in daily life, it is okay for them to cry in prison. Perhaps the combination of being more confined and more willing to express emotions leads to a unit in which there are more complaints, louder voices, and greater demands on staff.

When a staff member walks into 5-South, he or she is hit with a rush of activity and a barrage of languages. The unit is a microcosm of New York. Not only are there whites, blacks, Hispanics, and Asians, but there are subgroups of each. Hispanics are represented by Colombians, Puerto Ricans, Dominicans, and Cubans. Black groups include Afro-Americans, Nigerians, and a variety of other African groups. There is no culturally mixed unit like this one anywhere else in the federal system.

This diversity creates significant cultural and communication barriers, which is frustrating for the inmates who live together, as well as for staff members who ensure that the inmates receive proper care. A visitor may be approached by several inmates complaining (in their own languages) of aches, pains, or weight gain due to lack of exercise and demanding: "When can I see my kids?" "When can I get what I need in the commissary?" "Can you get in touch with my lawyer?" "Can you help me?" It's a unit where many of the inmates are forceful in their requests. Staff must be patient to understand and respond to their needs.

While male inmates tend to seek out counselors regarding phone call and visiting privileges, most of the female inmates complain about a lack of supplies, says 5-South Unit Manager Katherine Gant. "They never have enough underwear or uniforms, and the commissary doesn't sell specific feminine items." Gant also says additional staffing is needed on the women's unit because more time is necessary to handle their problems.

Since MCC New York is a holding facility for women immediately following arrest, many women have not had the chance to make provisions for child care. A typical problem women encounter is attempting to contact child welfare or other appropriate agencies to ensure proper guardianship of their children. Furthermore, a woman who is pregnant needs additional care, attention, and assistance. It may require thirty to forty minutes for a worker on the women's unit to work out just one problem, whereas a complaint from on the men's unit generally takes five to ten minutes to handle.

Psychological Concerns

The psychology staff also deals with inmate complaints and concerns and detect differences between complaints presented by men and women during therapeutic sessions. Generally, men discuss their fears and problems about being incarcerated, perhaps indicating a loss of power and independence. Female inmates talk more about their family, specifically their children and the guilt they feel over leaving them with others. According to Dr. Leslie Knutson, a staff psychologist at MCC New York, "Many of the women discuss the way they were abused in relationships and blame the men in their lives for manipulating them to get involved in illegal situations. They feel they are pawns in their relationships and are compelled to do what their boyfriend or husband tells them to. Their depression becomes more apparent as they verbalize their perceived victimization.''

At times their depression is so deep they have to be placed on a suicide watch. (Generally, they can be removed from a watch rather quickly because they are verbal about their feelings; the fact that they can vent their emotions leads to a quick resolution of their crisis.) This, however, is not the main reason for suicide watches among women at MCC New York. While most suicide watches among men occur immediately following incarceration as a result of their reaction to their arrest, most suicide watches among women occur after they have been incarcerated for a time. Most of these women have deep psychological problems that are exacerbated by the stress of prison life. In 1990, seven out of ten women placed on a suicide watch at MCC New York had serious psychological problems, such as psychosis. Two were suffering from severe depression that required antidepressant medication, and one suffered from a severe anxiety disorder that produced self-destructive behavior and pseudoseizures. Because of the seriousness of their illnesses, four of these inmates were put on a watch more than once.

The hospital staff is also very familiar with the complaints of female inmates. According to Douglas Reed, hospital administrator, ''There is a large number of female medical complaints, most of which center around minor aches and pains, gynecological problems, and sleep disturbance. In fact, one-quarter of sick call, on a routine basis is made up of women. Reed says this results from two factors: the women are seeking medical assistance that is not readily available to them outside prison, and they are seeking a little extra attention. Unfortunately, this extra attention takes up much of the physician assistants' time—more of their time is spent on 5-South than on any other unit. Furthermore, health care for women is more expensive than that provided for men. The Bureau of Prisons' hospital facility at Springfield, Missouri, can evaluate the general laboratory work for all inmates but cannot do so for some female tests, which must be sent to more costly local laboratories.

Managing Inmate Problems

Despite the stress of living on 5-South, many of the women are friendly and talkative and are helpful to other inmates who are experiencing problems. The women who make up the suicide watch team express a great deal of concern over troubled inmates, and at times they continue to watch distraught inmates even when the official watch is over. In an attempt to adjust to their isolation and emotional deprivation, some women form symbolic families in which they nurture other ''family'' members. Other inmates actually take on the role of mother, father, sister, brother, or child, as well as extended ''family'' members. This type of role-playing—an unhealthy form of dependency—is unique to women's institutions.

Many women participate in programs designed by staff at MCC New York to help them adjust to their initial time in prison. Women can work in the kitchen during the midnight shift when there is little or no movement in the institution. The education and recreation departments also provide special programs: drama, arts and crafts, English as a second language, and exercise. The psychology department has created several women's groups—drug abuse groups, groups for mothers, and a general therapy group. The hospital staff, in an attempt to respond to the increasing needs of the female population, has begun to provide monthly educational sessions on medical issues such as AIDS, breast cancer, and others.

If Shakespeare had seen 5-South he would never have suggested: "Frailty, thy name is woman." He would have emphasized the toughness and strength that make these women survivors. Despite the freedom of their surroundings—Wall Street, the South Street Seaport, and the Brooklyn Bridge—they are living in a confined space and adjusting to a variety of culturally diverse individuals as roommates, sometimes for months. Their toughness mirrors that of the officers who must face the daily challenges of this unit. Working on 5-South requires perseverance, patience, creativity, and diligence to maintain order in a potentially turbulent environment.

XVIII.

Canada's New Federal System for Female Offenders

by Jane Miller-Ashton

In March 1989, the commissioner of the Correctional Service of Canada (CSC), Ole Ingstrup, established the Task Force on Federally Sentenced Women in collaboration with the Canadian Association of Elizabeth Fry Societies (a nonprofit, private-sector organization that works with and on behalf of women in conflict with the law). The task force included female offenders, as well as members from a broad range of relevant community agencies, women's groups, aboriginal (native) organizations, and government departments. Many women participated in the task force, and decision making was conducted by consensus.

The task force was one of five created by the CSC to review such fundamental correctional issues as substance abuse, mental health, and community and institutional programs. The results are being used by CSC to more effectively address the needs of offenders in their efforts to become law-abiding citizens.

In April 1990, the Task Force on Federally Sentenced Women submitted its final report, which called for a new approach to meeting the unique needs of federally sentenced women.

At the time of the completion of the report, about 260 federally sentenced women were incarcerated in Canada, about 50 percent of whom were housed at the only Federal Prison for Women, a maximum security institution built in 1934 in Kingston, Ontario. Most of the others were serving their sentences in provincial institutions. There were, as well, about 200 women under community release supervision. The number of female offenders is generally stable and represents 2 percent of the total federal offender population in Canada.

Issues and Concerns

The following long-standing and unresolved issues have placed women, due in part to their small numbers, at a disadvantage in the correctional system:

- the geographic dislocation of many women from their families, cultures, and communities

Jane Miller-Ashton is the national coordinator for the Federally Sentenced Women's Initiative, Correctional Service of Canada.

- the overclassification of many women and the lack of significant opportunity for movement within a range of both institutional and community facilities and programs
- the lack of sufficient programs and services that respond to the unique needs of women
- program inequities that result from placing women in provincial institutions, which are often not geared to the needs of longer-term offenders
- the difficulty of effective prerelease planning
- the uniquely disadvantageous situation experienced by aboriginal women who, at about 16 percent, are overrepresented in the federal prison population and are particularly isolated from their cultures and communities

Over the years, these problems have been examined by a variety of task forces and commissions, and considerable effort has been made to improve the situation for federally sentenced women. Nonetheless, major problems have persisted. Numerous and recent recommendations to close the Federal Prison for Women emerged, challenges under the Charter of Rights were launched, and pressures for substantive change continued to mount from concerned lobby groups.

Given this background, the mandate of the task force was to examine the correctional management of federally sentenced women from the beginning of their sentences to the expiration of their warrants and to develop a plan to guide the process in a manner responsive to the unique needs of women.

Findings

The report of the Task Force on Federally Sentenced Women was based on insights gained from extensive consultations and from several research projects. Pertinent findings included the following:

- the hardship of mother-child separation expressed by incarcerated women, two-thirds of whom are mothers, and many of whom are single parents of children under five years of age
- the extensive histories of physical or sexual abuse experienced by 80 percent of the women and 90 percent of aboriginal women
- the high incidence of self-injurious behavior among women at the Prison for Women and its relationship to past histories of abuse
- the relatively high incidence of substance abuse as part of the offense or offense history of the women and their expressed need for more comprehensive substance abuse programs.
- the need for educational and vocational training geared to the development of marketable skills.
- the paucity of community-based services for federally sentenced women
- the need for culturally sensitive programs and services

- the desire expressed by federally sentenced women to be closer to home
- the evidence that successful programs for female offenders include those that focus on self-awareness and self-esteem, promote community involvement and adherence to community norms, use tools validated for women and aboriginal peoples, and provide supportive environments responsive to the needs of women with less emphasis on static security measures

Recommendations

The task force made eight short-term recommendations geared to improving the immediate situation at the Prison for Women. In large measure these recommendations have been fully implemented. In addition, an eleven-bed minimum security institution for federally sentenced women was opened during the course of deliberations.

The task force's longer-term plan incorporated a societal understanding of women's and aboriginal people's experience of disadvantage. It was based on the belief that a holistic female-centered approach to the treatment of federally sentenced women is required to address the historical problems and is predicated on principles of empowerment, meaningful choices, respect and dignity, supportive environments, and shared responsibility. The plan placed a high emphasis on the need for federally sentenced women to recover from past trauma and to develop self-esteem and self-sufficiency through programs and services designed to respond to their needs. It stressed the need for physical environments that are conducive to reintegration, are highly interactive with the community, and reflect the generally low security risk of these women.

The plan included the following recommendations:

1. Close the Prison for Women.
2. Establish four federally operated regional facilities for federally incarcerated women.
3. Establish a healing lodge that would serve as an incarceration option for federally sentenced aboriginal women.
4. Develop a community release strategy that would expand and strengthen residential and nonresidential programs and services for women on release.
5. Respond to the needs of the few women from remote or northern parts of Canada by negotiating agreements for them to remain in their home areas under territorial/provincial jurisdiction.

The task force plan was situated within the Canadian federal government's ongoing efforts to achieve equality for women and aboriginal people and was fundamentally rooted in the mission of CSC, which respects the dignity of individuals, the rights of all members of society, and the potential for human growth and development. It was consistent with CSC's strategic objectives to provide a safe, humane environment that promotes health and well-being and encourages positive interaction between offenders and staff. Further, it honored CSC policy respecting the social, cultural, and religious differences of individual offenders and addressed the special needs of female and native offenders. Finally, the plan brought a disadvantaged group within a long-standing CSC policy of regionalization, enhancing program opportunities for women and bringing them closer to their families, communities, and cultures.

The locations recommended by the task force report for the regional facilities were based on proximity to the home communities of the majority of women from a given region and on the availability of community resources generally found in larger urban centers.

Facility Description

The task force recommended that regional facilities be developed and operated on a program philosophy that approximates community norms, focuses on extensive use of community expertise, and is geared to the safe release of federally sentenced women at the earliest possible point in their sentences. Program delivery would be based on gender-sensitive assessments and individualized plans developed by each woman in conjunction with a staff person (primary support worker) and a community worker assigned from a private-sector agency.

Programs should be holistic, culturally sensitive, and responsive to the needs of women. Primary programming would focus on counseling and treatment, including sexual, physical, and substance abuse recovery; educational, vocational, and skills development; leisure activities; family visitation; on-site residence of children; and spiritual services. Self-sufficiency and community responsibility would be fostered through daily opportunities for living skills acquisition and through the positive support of staff who are skilled in counseling, communicating, and negotiating and are sensitive to women's and cross-cultural issues.

It was recommended that the regional facilities be situated on several acres of land and be built to modern environmental standards that foster wellness, including considerations of natural light, fresh air, color, space, and privacy. Living areas would be cottage-style, with six to eight women per cottage. A central core area for administration would contain flexible program space for recreational, social, spiritual, and counseling activities. The facilities would be designed to maximize mother-child interaction and family visits.

The task force report suggested using dynamic rather than static security measures wherever possible to reflect the supportive orientation of the facilities. Unobtrusive security measures, for detection purposes only, were recommended to be added to what would otherwise be a boundary fence surrounding each facility, built to community standards. One cottage (or part of a cottage) in each facility would require enhanced static security features, but staff support to higher risk women would be the primary approach.

The task force recommended that the healing lodge be developed and operated according to native traditions and staffed by aboriginal men and women. The lodge would be designed in consultation with aboriginal people and would require, in addition to standard CSC administrative requirements, a connection to a nearby native community and the support of an elders' council. The physical space and programs for the healing lodge would reflect aboriginal culture. The needs of federally sentenced aboriginal women would be addressed through native teachings, ceremonies, contact with elders and children, and interaction with nature. Program delivery, as in the other facilities, would be premised on individualized plans, a holistic approach, an interactive relationship with the community, and a focus on release preparation. The healing lodge, however, would at all times operate from a unique cultural perspective, placing a high value on spiritual leadership, as well as on role modeling and the life experiences of staff, with more traditional professional expertise providing a largely supportive role.

Regional Advisory Councils

The task force report recommended that regional advisory councils be established in association with each regional facility to advise the CSC on the development and operation of programs and services in both the facility and the community.

Membership for the regional advisory councils would be drawn from local private-sector groups and individuals who have expertise and interest in women's issues and criminal justice. With respect to the healing lodge, the regional advisory council would take the form of both an elders' council and a connection to a local native community.

Councils would evaluate existing programs, identify gaps in services, and recommend additional programs and services. They would also monitor the continuity of programs between the facility and community and make recommendations on how continuity could be improved. Finally, councils would play an educational role in their local communities so that the facility and the women released from it are seen as an integral part, and a responsibility, of the community.

Community Release Strategy

As envisioned by the task force report, the community orientation of the regional facilities would facilitate the development of individualized release plans, assisted by a community support team. The team, composed of CSC staff and community workers, would work closely with each woman to ensure that needed services would be available on release.

This effort would be supported by new, enhanced residential and nonresidential opportunities for women. There would be an increased need for specialized services, including aboriginal halfway houses and community-based treatment residences, as well as alternate accommodations such as satellite apartment beds and private home placements. Services purchased from community residential facilities would include employment counseling, substance abuse treatment, and living skills programs.

Implementation

In September 1990 the government announced the acceptance of the task force's major recommendations. Included in the acceptance were plans to close the Prison for Women by fall 1994, to establish the five new facilities, and to expand and enhance community services and programs for federally sentenced women. The construction cost is estimated to be about $50 million in Canadian currency.

In October 1990, the commissioner of corrections announced the creation of a National Implementation Committee to oversee the initiative—including all operational input to the planning and development of the regional facilities, the healing lodge, and the community strategy.

In December 1990, an External Advisory Committee was established to provide advice on the overall initiative. The committee includes members from Status of Women Canada (a federal government department), the Canadian Association of Elizabeth Fry Societies, and the Native Women's Association of Canada. In February 1991, a healing lodge planning committee composed of representatives from aboriginal women's groups, native elders, and CSC staff was established to plan the healing lodge. The high representation of native partners on this committee is unique and reflects the importance of ensuring that this facility is culturally sensitive.

Site Selection

During the months following the government's acceptance, an unprecedented number of communities expressed an interest in having the facilities located in their areas. In July 1991, Solicitor General Doug Lewis announced that the new facilities would be located within 100 kilometers of the major centers of Halifax, Montreal, Toronto, and Edmonton or Calgary.

The Correctional Service of Canada subsequently developed selection criteria, and communities were given an opportunity to submit proposals based on those criteria. Forty-four communities were assessed by members of the National Implementation Committee that also included a staff member from Status of Women Canada. A report was submitted to the solicitor general in early December 1991, and later that month he announced plans to locate the Atlantic facility in Truro, Nova Scotia, and the Ontario facility in Kitchener. Announcements for the Quebec and Alberta facilities are expected in the near future.

There is no requirement for a regional facility in British Columbia because federal women are now housed in a new provincial facility for women in that province. This agreement was negotiated prior to the task force report.

With respect to the healing lodge, the solicitor general announced that this facility would be established in the Province of Saskatchewan. This centrally located prairie province is home to many native women. The healing lodge committee subsequently developed culturally sensitive selection criteria to help determine the location for the healing lodge.

In March 1992, twenty-three Saskatchewan communities (many of them joint partnership proposals from urban centers and nearby aboriginal communities) were evaluated. The first-place submission from Maple Creek/Nekaneet in Saskatchewan was endorsed by the solicitor general and made public on 22 May 1992. This community was selected because of its strong aboriginal qualifications: sacred land, pure spring water, and the support of a traditional aboriginal community, including elders and medicine people. In addition, this community was favored because of the harmonious relationship that seemed to exist between the native and non-native citizens.

Operational Plan

In addition to determining geographic locations, the National Implementation Committee has developed an operational plan for the new facilities. Because the new approach to federally sentenced women will, in some cases, mark a significant departure from existing policy and practice, it was deemed important to develop a plan that would provide a framework to ensure some commonality and consistency among the new women's facilities. The operational plan was developed in consultation with private-sector partners and other CSC staff and with input from female offenders themselves. The plan reflects the principles of the task force report, as well as the knowledge about women in prison gained through consultation and research. Similarly, the warden's job description for the new facilities and the selection process for these individuals has been developed to capture the unique aspects of management in this type of setting. Other aspects of facility development will receive similar attention to ensure sensitivity to women's issues as the planning progresses.

Conclusion

The undertaking in Canada parallels initiatives taking place in other jurisdictions to promote positive change for women in prison. The unique aspects of the Canadian experience, which appear to have worked successfully, relate to the significant involvement and consultation with female offenders; the partnership developed with private-sector groups, including aboriginal peoples; and the commitment of the Correctional Service of Canada and the Canadian Federal Government to make needed changes for incarcerated women.

Other Titles Available from ACA

The Female Offender: What Does the Future Hold?

This book documents an incisive survey taken by the ACA Task Force on the Female Offender. Highlights information about the dramatic increase in the number of female offenders, facility design and location, demographics, security issues, and much more. It also includes recommendations for dealing with the problems associated with the growing female population. *(1990, 112 pages)*

As Free as an Eagle

Daniel J. Bayse

A survival guide for inmates and their families, this straightforward book examines the complex issues and problems families must face during incarceration and after release. It teaches the offender how to establish productive relationships, develop problem-solving skills, and reenter society on release in a self-help styled format. *(1991, 235 pages)*

Getting High and Doing Time:
What's the Connection? A Recovery Guide for Alcoholics and
Drug Addicts in Trouble with the Law

Edward M. Read, LCSW, CAC, and Dennis C. Daley, MSW

A workbook-style guide aimed at emphasizing to readers the implications of their substance abuse problems. It explores the definition and causes of addiction and promotes a better understanding of addiction through true-life accounts from recovering alcoholics and addicts. A useful self-help counseling tool for inmates incarcerated within a facility, and also probationers and parolees. *(1990, 88 pages)*

Helping Hands: A Handbook for Volunteers in Prisons and Jails

Daniel J. Bayse

A practical guide for volunteers in correctional settings. The criminal justice system, security issues, understanding the criminal personality, communicating with inmates, and inmate slang are discussed. *(1992, 72 pages)*

Call 1-800-825-2665 for more information about these and other ACA publications